Your guide to the

STRANGEST
MUSEUMS IN BRITAIN

- and the best worldwide -

FRONT COVER PICTURES

top left - Salem Witch Museum - page 50
top right - Icelandic Phallological Museum - page 76
bottom left - Lawnmower Museum - page 27
bottom right - Dog Collar Museum - page 29

STRANGEST

MUSEUMS IN BRITAIN

- and the best worldwide -

TITLE NUMBER 4. FIRST EDITION.

WRITTEN & PUBLISHED BY
STRANGEST BOOKS

ACKNOWLEDGEMENTS

Thanks are given to those people who have kindly provided some of the photographs for inclusion
in this book. These photographs are reproduced with the permission of the relevant copyright holders.
Certain images appear from public domain.

This book is the result of extensive research and the entries contained herein are inserted at the sole
discretion of the publishers. This does not indicate a preference over establishments not included.
The publishers receive no payments or inducements for inclusion in this book.

foreword

Most of us can clearly remember a time when we saw or read about something that was so strange or unusual it made us gasp in wonder, or even sent a cold chill through our body.

The Strangest series of Books has the very best compilations of all that is weird, amazing and bizarre in Britain (and the rest of the world) today, and will open up a wonderland of curiosities for you to discover - most of which you probably never knew existed.

Each of the books in our series covers a chosen subject and will provide you with a thoroughly entertaining read. There are fascinating, mysterious, and very often unbelievable places and things to be seen. Some are so unusual that only a visit to actually see for yourself will suffice, or you can simply experience an unforgettable bedtime read, and then amaze your friends and colleagues with some of the startling facts.

Sure to provide readers with as much pleasure as they did for the researchers, the Strangest series of Books can be purchased or ordered from all good book stores and high street retailers. Information on how to order direct can be found on page 96.

The more that you read, the more things you will know.

The more that you learn, the more places you'll go.

- Dr Seuss

about this book

There are so many museums worldwide that a definitive book published on the subject would be too heavy to lift. The curiosity that is instilled within us all means that people take great enjoyment from wandering around collections in museums - from the most impressive history museums, the latest science museums, and even the small specialist museums that are quite often found tucked away up some little side street.

There are collections of just about everything imaginable to be seen in museums throughout the world, and to discover the truly unusual and strange then this book - Strangest Museums in Britain *and the best worldwide* , will tell you where to find them and what you will see. Can there really be an international toilet museum, or a museum for the crutches of cured patients? Or what about the hair museum or the bizarre parasite museum.

Outrageous museums of all types and descriptions such as asparagus, mummies, and barbed wire museums. How about a paper airplane museum, a voodoo museum, or - believe it or not - a penis museum. Our favourites? Must be the lawnmower museum and the sex museum. From the mildly eccentric to the truly insane, they are all here in a book you will want to read more than once - Strangest Museums in Britain *and the best worldwide.*

alphabetical index of entries

Part One - BRITAIN

Part Two - USA

COLORADO
Museum of Colorado Prisons - gas chambers and cannibals - page 64

GEORGIA
Lunchbox Museum - 1,000 of them to see - page 42

HAWAII
Paper Airplane Museum - world's only paper airplane museum - page 62

KANSAS
The Kansas Barbed Wire Museum - yes, you've read it correctly - page 46

LOUISIANA
New Orleans Historic Voodoo Museum - magic and mystery with voodoo - page 41

MARYLAND
American Visionary Art Museum - art that makes sense or non-sense? - page 55
Decoy Museum - 2,800 decoy ducks, they must be quackers - page 66
National Cryptologic Museum - codemakers and codebreakers - page 56

MASSACHUSETTS
The American Sanitary Plumbing Museum - weird and wacky - page 48
The Salem Witch Museum - witchcraft trials & not for the faint hearted - page 49

MINNESOTA
Museum of Questionable Medical Devices - as the name states - page 58

MISSOURI
Leila's Hair Museum - the human hair museum - page 40

NEW HAMPSHIRE
Museum of Family Camping - relive your wanderlust years - page 70

NEW MEXICO
International UFO Museum & Research Centre - alien sightings - page 50

NEW YORK
Jell-O Museum - the jelly emporium - page 43
Museum of Sex - porn, porn, and more porn - page 68
Sing Sing Prison Museum - notorious prison still occupied - page 64
The Skyscraper Museum - the evolution of tall buildings - page 51

NORTH CAROLINA
Belhaven Memorial Museum - an 8-legged pig & a 2-headed kitten - page 53

OKLAHOMA
National Lighter Museum - 30,000 fire starters on display - page 45

PENNSYLVANIA
Mister Ed's Elephant Museum - elephants of all descriptions - page 60
Mutter Museum - 27ft human colon and a woman made from soap - page 39

SOUTH DAKOTA
Ghosts of Deadwood Gulch Wax Museum - Wild Bill Hickok's death chair - page 61
The International Vinegar Museum - includes paper made from vinegar - page 63

TENNESSEE
Salt & Pepper Shaker Museum - 17,000 condiment containers - page 63

TEXAS
Barney Smith's Toilet Seat Art Museum - 700 outrageously decorated seats - page 48
Buckhorn Saloon & Museum - must be seen to be believed - page 61
Devil's Rope Museum - unbelievable but true - page 46
National Museum of Funeral History - hearses and coffins of all kinds - page 57
Texas Prison Museum - see Old Sparky where 361 prisoners were 'fried' - page 64
The Conspiracy Museum - who killed JFK? - page 51

VIRGINIA
Drug Enforcement Administration Museum - opium, crack and marijuana - page 67
John Q.Adams Centre for the history of Otolaryngology - head/neck surgery - page 67

WISCONSIN
Mount Horeb Mustard Museum - a hot place to visit - page 62
Museum of Woodcarving - must be seen - page 66

WYOMING
National Atomic Museum - all about atomic bombs - page 45

Part Three - REST OF WORLD

AUSTRIA
The Bell Museum - your sure to clap here - page 90

AZERBAIJAN
Napthalan Museum for the Crutches of Cured Patients - unbelievable - page 90

CANADA
Criminals Hall of Fame Wax Museum - bloody exhibits - page 79
The Bata Shoe Museum - striking and unusual shoe collection - page 87

CHINA
Museum of Qin Terra Cotta Warriors and Horses - 8th wonder of the world - page 80

COSTA RICA
Museo Criminologico - gruesome to say the least - page 79

DENMARK
Bottle Peter Museum - 750 ships in bottles - page 91

FRANCE
Paris Sewers Museum - tour of the turd tunnels - page 94

GERMANY
Cultural History of the Hand Museum - hands used in all possible ways - page 83
European Asparagus Museum - tips on the 'royal vegetable' - page 86
German Hygeine Museum - fascinating museum - page 83
Sewer Museum - you won't believe what's found in sewers - page 94
Zeppelin Museum - airships museum - page 95

HOLLAND
Amsterdam Sex Museum - erotic, exotic, and full of sex - page 92

ICELAND
The Icelandic Phallogical Museum - every willie there is - page 76

INDIA
Sulabh International Museum of Toilets - high temple of the loo - page 73

ITALY
National Museum of Pasta Foods - spaghetti bolognese for all - page 75
Salvatore Ferragamo Shoe Museum - 10,000 weird shoes, many bizarre - page 87

JAPAN
Beppu Hihokan - explicit Japanese sex palace - page 88
Meiji University Museum of Criminology - being a crook in Japan - page 79
Shin-Yokohama Ramen Museum - noodle emporium - page 75
The Laundry Museum - washday blues - page 72
The Meguro Parasitological Museum - 300 horrendous parasites - page 89
Tobacco & Salt Museum - very quirky museum - page 82

MEXICO
Guanajuato Mummy Museum - 107 gruesome modern mummies - page 84

Part One
- BRITAIN -

The Sherlock Holmes Museum in London - page 34.

Artifacts from a bygone era on show at The Cumberland Pencil Museum in Keswick, the place where pencils were first made.

THE CUMBERLAND PENCIL MUSEUM

Southey Works, Greta Bridge, Keswick, Cumbria
Tel: 01768 773626

Following the discovery of graphite the first pencils ever made were produced in Keswick by hand. Starting with a piece of graphite which was then sawn into slabs, a piece of wood was then grooved with a square groove. The slab of graphite was inserted into the groove, indented, and broken off level with the top of the groove. A thin slat of wood was then glued to the top which left the graphite encased. Many families in Keswick made these pencils in their cottages (hence the saying "cottage industry") and all the work was carried out by hand. Today, pencils are mass produced by machinery, and a journey through the Cumberland Pencil Museum will enable you to discover not only the history of pencil making but also artistic techniques, workshops, machinery displays, and much more.

Of particular interest is the longest pencil in the world on permanent display in the museum. At 7.91 metres in length (over 25ft), it weighs in at an astonishing 446 kilos (984lb). Amongst other items to be seen is a special pencil that was issued to World War II pilots. It was intended to assist their escape from prisoner-of-war camps and part of the lead has been replaced with a map of Germany, and a tiny compass sits underneath the eraser on the end. A day out at The Cumberland Pencil Museum is sure to interest all the family. Put some lead in your pencil lad!

Graphite is one of the physical forms in which the element carbon is found. Graphite was first discovered in the Seathwaite Valley on the side of the mountain Seathwaite Fell in Borrowdale, Cumbria around the year 1500. The story relates that shepherds went out in the morning following a particularly violent storm and found huge piles of black material where trees had been uprooted due to the storm. The shepherds thought it was coal, but the value of the material was soon discovered and the Government took over the site. The graphite was transported to London by stage-coach and it soon became popular for medicinal purposes, with another use being as moulds in the manufacture of cannon balls.

When pencils were first produced following the discovery of graphite, its fame quickly spread. Flemish traders touted it as a most useful material to artists all over the world and it was first used as rough pieces wrapped in sheepskin. The Italians first developed a wooden holder. The shape of the knife in the plane determined whether a pencil was oval, round or square, and later on small foot-operated lathes were introduced.

THE BOOT AND SHOE COLLECTION

Northampton Museum & Art Gallery, Guildhall Road, Northampton, Northamptonshire
Tel: 01604 838111

This world famous collection of boots and shoes contains over 12,000 items ranging from ancient Egyptian material to modern designs. It is said to be the largest collection in the world and includes not only boots and shoes but also accessories such as buckles, laces, shoe-horns, etc. There are shoemaking tools and machines, masses of documentary material, decorative art including paintings and prints depicting shoes and the shoemaking industry, and even an index of shoemakers and shoemaking firms from the Roman period onwards.

The Life & Sole gallery shows the history of shoemaking in addition to a recreation of a Northampton shoe factory. Those of you who are superstitious may want to view the Index of Concealed Shoes which is a listing of shoes hidden in buildings to bring good luck.

ROYAL NAVY SUBMARINE MUSEUM

Haslar Jetty Road, Gosport, Hampshire. Tel: 02392 529217

This unique museum provides the opportunity to go aboard a real submarine and is a fascinating insight of what life must have been like living in cramped conditions hundreds of feet below the surface of the sea. Your visit will include a film show, a guided tour of HMS Alliance, a view of Portsmouth Harbour through the periscopes of HMS Conqueror, and a look at the large collection of submarines and torpedoes.

The museum houses over 4,000 objects in a varied collection that includes medals, uniforms, relics, art, weapons, flags, and a whole lot more. There are 17 periscopes on display, and some of the personal effects to be seen includes items that represent a submariner's everyday life whilst at sea - games, cigarette cases, suitcases, even belongings of prisoners of war are represented.

The weapons collection is particularly interesting and illustrates the development of submarine weaponry from the 1890's to the present day. Torpedoes, torpedo calculators, mines, firearms, and even Polaris and Tomahawk missiles can be seen. Careful what you bump into here.

The collection of flags is another must see. The unique 'Jolly Roger', ensigns and commissioning pennants, and Rear Admiral's flags make up part of this collection.

The Royal Navy Submarine Museum also charts the history of submarine development from the times of Alexander the Great to the present day, and the history of the British Submarine Service; from a miniscule submarine to the mighty nuclear powered Vanguard class submarine, the vessel in use by the Navy today.

DALI UNIVERSE
County Hall Gallery, Riverside Building, County Hall, London SE1. Tel: 0870 744 7485

The permanent Dali Universe exhibition here is a surreal visit into the mind of Salvador Dali, the great creative genius of the 20th century. More than 500 of his works are exhibited in an amazing world of melting clocks and bizarre sculptures that amuse and amaze in equal proportions. Created by Beniamino Levi, who worked with Salvador on most of his sculptures, the exhibition attracts hundreds of thousands of visitors every year and is a place you simply must see on a visit to the capital. Located on the South Bank.

THE DOG COLLAR MUSEUM
Leeds Castle, Maidstone, Kent. Tel: 01622 765400

It had to come. With museums on just about everything imaginable out there this one is the latest in a long line of the very unusual. Dog collars is the subject and dog collars you see. Over 100 of them - plus related items - all on display in the historic setting of Leeds Castle Gatehouse in Kent. The collection was donated to the Leeds Castle Foundation by Mrs Gertrude Hunt in memory of her husband, John Hunt, the distinguished medievalist. Why Leeds Castle you may think? Well, dogs have always been an important part of life at the Castle; huge mastiffs that once guarded the gates, gundogs and hounds for hunting, and lap-dogs to grace the apartments of queens.

The exhibits include broad iron collars that have fearsome spikes jutting out of them. These were in use from the 15th century onwards and were designed to protect the throats of hunting dogs from attacks by wolves, bears and wild boar. The impressive collection has been added to since its donation and items of superb artistic craftmanship can be seen such as the German and Austrian Baroque leather collars from the 17th and 18th centuries, decorated with intricate metalwork and velvet.

The only one of its kind in Britain, The Dog Collar Museum is well worth visiting, if only to see what your hound is missing out on.

Some ancient collars, and protective hunting collars. Part of the dog collar collection on show at Leeds Castle.

THE PSYCHIC MUSEUM
35 Stonegate, York, Yorkshire
Tel: 01904 622864

York is one of the most historic cities you will ever visit and is also said to be Britain's most haunted city. Once home to Romans and Vikings there is a plethora of attractions to see including the awe-inspiring Minster, the Jorvik Viking Centre, and the city walls. One of the latest attractions to be opened in this beautiful city is The Psychic Museum, the brainchild of astrologer Jonathon Cainer and psychic celebrity spoon-bender Uri Geller.

The building the museum is housed in is itself over 600 years old and includes many original and impressive features including rooms with oak panelling. It stands on a site that has been occupied continuously since 71AD and prior to conversion into a museum was in the hands of a family of artisans for over 120 years.

The museum seeks to encourage interest in psychic phenomena and to teach people that there are such things as a 'sixth sense', extrasensory perception, and perhaps even telekinesis.

Upon arrival you and your fellow travellers for the journey of exploration you will undertake are introduced to your guide. In each room you visit you will witness amazing experiments and also find out if you yourself possess any hidden powers. Dowsing, energy fields, remote viewing, telepathy, and psychokinesis are all explored in a fascinating and hugely entertaining tour. Step into the unknown at this most unique museum, in this most unique building.

CUCKOOLAND
The Old School, Chester Road, Tabley, Cheshire
Tel: 01565 633039

Welcome to the only cuckoo clock museum in the world. Put together over 30 years, this collection is regarded as the most important of its kind anywhere and contains rare, unique, and some highly unusual methods of time telling. Assembled by noted horologists and clock restorers, brothers Roman and Maz Piekarski, the collection contains some of the rarest cuckoo clocks in the world which have been lovingly restored to their former splendour. Having sought out clocks worldwide to make good and preserve for heritage and the benefit of future generations, they have dedicated their lives to maintaining and improving the collection.

This particular clockmaking craft originated in the Black Forest region of Central Europe when natural materials from the forest were used. Skills developed over the years and the bellowsmaker developed the sound by including 2 small bellows of goat-kid skin that blew into 2 small flutes. Other craftsmen worked on the casework, face, hands and numerals, and mechanism.

The museum also has Quail clocks, Trumpeter clocks, and other musical movements in addition to Black Forest Fairground organs that play marches and dance-hall music.

Cuckoo clocks may also be purchased here and this is certainly a day out with a pleasant difference.

- grassed up -

THE BRITISH LAWNMOWER MUSEUM
106-114 Shakespeare Road, Southport, Lancashire
Tel: 01704 501336

This family operated business started in 1945 and is the culmination of a dream by ex racing champion Brian Radam. His interest in this type of equipment started in 1945 and it has now mushroomed into an internationally famous museum and one of the worlds foremost authorities on vintage lawnmowers, becoming the largest import and export specialist in antique garden machinery, and supplying parts, materials, and valuation services all over the world. Apart from the museum, The Discount Garden Machinery Warehouse Stanleys side of the business caters for all aspects of sales, spares and service.

The museum workshops restores machines for its collection and also for vintage garden machinery for lawnmower enthusiasts and collectors. Included in the unique collection that can be seen at the museum are some of the fastest lawnmowers in the world which have been featured on television, the water cooled 'Egg Boiler' lawnmower, a genuine '2 inch' lawnmower, the most expensive lawnmower in the world, and the first solar powered robot mower.

Lawnmowers of the rich and famous are also displayed here such as those that have previously seen service in the esteemed company of Prince Charles, Hilda Ogden of Coronation Street fame, Alan Titchmarsh, Nicholas Parsons, and many more.

The first Atco and Ransome lawnmowers seen here are notables within the lawnmower industry, and the collection includes items made by manufacturers not normally associated with the garden industry such as Daimler, Hawker Sidley, Rolls Royce, and British Leyland, to name but a few.

Since opening, the museum has attracted interest globally, which is hardly surprising as in addition to all the above it also boasts machines that date back to the invention of the lawnmower in the 1830's, and has the largest collection of toy lawnmowers in the world.

I couldn't tell the front from the back of these machines - the wife mows our garden.

THE HELICOPTER MUSEUM
Locking Moor Road, Weston-Super-Mare, Somerset
Tel: 01934 635227

Up, up and away at The Helicopter Museum where assorted helicopters and related artifacts can be seen. Its origins go back to 1958 when the founder, aviation writer Elfan ap Rees, started to build a private collection of rotorcraft items and documentation. In 1969 he acquired his first complete helicopter, a Bristol Sycamore Mk.3. More acquisitions were made over the years and the collection now includes rare prototypes such as the Campbell Cougar Autogyro and the Fairey Ultra-Light. Welcome to the world's largest dedicated helicopter museum.

*Vintage lawnmowers and
vintage helicopters - two
very different means of travel.*

BANK OF ENGLAND MUSEUM
Threadneedle Street, London EC2. Tel: 0207 601 4878

The Bank of England has issued banknotes for in excess of 300 years and The Bank of England Museum tells the story from its foundation in 1694 up to the present time as the central bank of the United Kingdom. The displays here will encourage you to have that extra line on the lottery this week as the modern and Roman gold bars shimmer in a golden light.

Pikes and muskets which were once used to defend the bank from potential robbers sit alongside historical displays that include silver, banknotes, coins and fine prints. Books, documents, and many photographs chart the bank's past together with its present and future commitment to maintaining financial stability as it sets interest rates to control inflation. Everyday items associated with banking such as keys, seals and balance weights can be seen, but the collection of banknotes is quite unique and includes original artwork by note designers and a highly impressive collection of the best forgeries to be produced and found in circulation. In fact this is the largest collection of Bank of England banknotes and associated material in the world.

Statues and busts including one of William Pitt the Younger watch over you, and the obligatory museum shop offers a range of exclusive Bank of England goodies to take home. Nice as they are I'd prefer a gold bar.

MUSEUM OF ARMY CHAPLAINCY
Amport House, Amport, Andover, Hampshire
Tel: 01264 773144

Housing the archives and historic relics of RAChD (Royal Army Chaplains Department) and its chaplains, the displays here illustrate the story of Army Chaplaincy in all its uses; captivity, war, and teaching the faith. Visitors will not find any arms or weapons here since the chaplains were non-combatants with a duty to the service of peace. What can be seen is a poignant look at uniforms, prisoner-of-war items, militaty items including badges and insignia, and the stories of the chaplains who have been awarded the Victoria Cross. The shop offers a selection of memorabilia and general gifts.

BLACKED-OUT BRITAIN WAR MUSEUM
1 St Marys Street, Huntingdon, Cambridgeshire
Tel: 01480 450998

This is a museum that tells you all about what life was really like in the dark years from 1939 to 1945 when Britain was at war. Rationing was a sufferance that was forced upon almost everyone and memorabilia here includes ration books, dried eggs, and a whole lot more - even bombs. See what it was really like on the Home Front at the Blacked-Out Britain War Museum.

EDEN CAMP
Malton, Ryedale, Yorkshire
Tel: 01653 697777

Said to be the only modern history theme museum of its type in the world Eden Camp is a comprehensive and compelling look at World War II that features an original prisoner-of-war camp built in 1942. Over 6 acres comprise this award winning museum which has over 30 huts and mess rooms to explore. The Home Front, War News Room, The Blitz, Women at War, The Rise of Hitler, The U-Boat Menace, and Britain Prepares are merely a few of them.

Reconstructed scenes include lighting, sound, movement and smells, to provide the feeling that you are actually there and taking part in history. The large collection of World War II operational vehicles means you can see a T34 Tank, Bren Gun Carrier, a Green Goddess, and an MK3 Hurricane amongst others.

This is a museum unlike any other and will take at least 3-4 hours to explore. Try the Prisoners Canteen or the Officers Mess. The Assault Course is designed for younger visitors, and there is even a miniature one for little Commandoes

OLD OPERATING THEATRE & HERB GARRET MUSEUM
9a St.Thomas's Street,
London SE1. Tel: 0207 188 2679

The Old Operating Theatre & Herb Garret Museum can be found at the top of a spiral staircase in the cavernous roof space of St.Thomas's Church. The Church was built by Wren's master mason, Thomas Cartwright.

The Old Operating Theatre, which was rediscovered in the 1950's after decades of neglect, has been lovingly restored and features much original furniture including a 19th century operating table. Stark, cold, and a grim reminder of the harsh realities of surgery prior to modern technology, this would have witnessed the screams of countless pour souls who either survived the sheer terror of having a limb brutally sawed off without anaesthetic, or died under operating conditions that were barbaric to say the least.

This is the only surviving 19th century operating theatre in the country and displays here include many surgical instruments such as those used for bleeding, child-birth and cupping, and the history of surgery and several hospitals. Also to be seen here is the history of herbal medicine and displays on medieval monastic health care.

The Old Operating Theatre & Herb Garret Museum is certainly a hidden treasure and is well worth visiting. Take a couple of Aspirin or Paracetamol if it all gets too much for you!

When St.Thomas's Church was rebuilt around 1703 a large oak beamed garret was discovered in the loft space. This had been used by St.Thomas's Apothecary (whose shop and offices were just along the street) to store and cure herbs - presumably as a garret (or attic) was less vulnerable to rats which were the plague of London at that time. A garret also provided a drier environment. During the restoration work 4 poppies were found in the garret, and as poppies are used in the preparation of opium the medical connection was confirmed.

The unusually large garret was converted into an operating theatre as it afforded a degree of soundproofing from the main wards of St.Thomas's Hospital - which were built around St.Thomas's Church. In those days it would have been an ideal place to demonstrate surgical skills as it had a large skylight above, and apprentice apothecaries had excellent vantage points in addition to a separate entrance. It also alleviated the terror that must have been felt by many patients who were witness to the screams that accompanied operations previously carried out on the wards. Until 1847 surgeons did not have the use of anaesthetics and operating speed was important. Alcohol or opiates would be used to mildly numb the patient's senses before cumbersome instruments were used to operate - or amputate - often completed within a minute or so.

An early 19th century operating table set in the middle of the Old Operating Theatre at the Herb Garret.

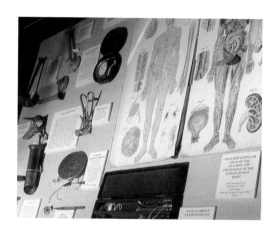

Anatomy charts and early medical memorabilia and (below), could it possibly be a preserved brain?

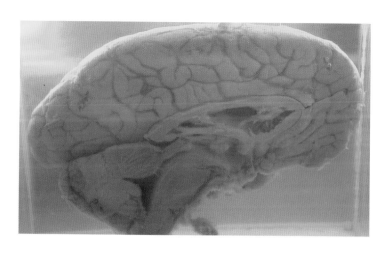

THE BAR CONVENT

**17 Blossom Street, York,
Yorkshire. Tel: 01904 643238**

The Bar Convent is located in a
Georgian building close to the centre of
historic York and houses a fascinating
museum outlining the early history of
Christianity in the north of England.
Mary Ward, who founded a religious
congregation, was a pioneer of women's
education and apostolic religious orders
for women. Her life story is related at
The Bar Convent in a series of pictures
which are reproduced in the museum.

Steeped in history, The Bar Convent
is the oldest existing Catholic Convent
in England having been established in
1686 by Frances Bedingfield, an early
member of Mary Ward's Institute. The
neo-classical chapel here was
completed in 1769 and has many
features which illustrate the penal times
during which it was built. Catholic
worship was forbidden at that time so
the chapel was constructed in the
centre of the complex of buildings,
having 8 exits by which the
congregation could escape in the event
of a raid by magistrates. The chapel is
still in daily use and also holds a weekly
mass.

Interestingly, this working convent
offers accommodation, has catering and
conference facilities, in addition to
having an extensive library and
archives. The Bar Convent Museum, as
well as The Bar Convent itself, offers
visitors the opportunity for
contemplation and reflection, and is a
true oasis amid the hustle and bustle of
busy York centre. Admission to the
Museum, Gallery and Chapel, is free to
all visitors.

HM CUSTOMS & EXCISE NATIONAL MUSEUM

**Albert Dock, Liverpool,
Merseyside
Tel: 01653 697777**

There is much to see and a lot to talk
about at HM Customs & Excise National
Museum which has any number of
curious and fascinating objects on
display, each of which explains a part of
the perpetual efforts by Customs
Officers to obtain levies due to the
Government.

Illicit trade was once rife all over the
country and at the museum you can
discover some of the most notorious
smugglers and their gangs such as The
Hawkhurst Gang who terrorised the
South Coast in the 1740's, and George
Moore, a seemingly respected merchant
from the Isle of Man.

Activities here include a 'search for
modern contraband' and 'spot the
smuggler'. In addition, you can see how
collecting duties was carried out in the
past, explore revenue collection as it is
today, and see some of the highlights of
the amazing collection of goods -
including fakes - that have been seized
over the years. Endangered species,
drugs, and other aspects of smuggling
are on the agenda here, and this is
certainly a museum with a difference.

COLLECTORS WORLD OF ERIC ST JOHN-FOTI

Hermitage Hall, Bridge Farm, Downham Market, Norfolk
Tel: 01366 383185

Said to be one of the most eccentric collectors in Britain and certainly the most prolific in Norfolk, the extraordinary lifetime collections which Eric St John-Foti amassed can be seen in a beautiful setting west of Downham Market. Collectors World is a vast place which quite literally takes your breath away. Amongst the numerous themed rooms to vist are The Pink Room, the Tapestry Room, the Ghosts of East Anglia Room, the Sixties Room, and The Chapel. The Pink Room is a tribute to the late Barbara Cartland and has probably the biggest collection of original associated memorabilia to be seen anywhere. Dresses, jewellery, photographs, manuscripts and much more is on show.

Nelson's death mask.

The Sixties Room has a mass of original material from this swinging era both from bands and individual singers. Also to be seen here are tape recorders, gramophones, radios and televisions from that time.

Horatio Nelson, one of the most famous ship captain's in the world, also has a room dedicated to him here. As he was educated in Downham Market and learned to sail on the nearby River Ouse, local people have a great affinity with him. See his personal belongings, maritime items, and even his death mask.

There is also an interesting Car & Aero Museum amongst the myriad of attractions to be seen at Collectors World. Rolls Royce Aero Engines, Armstrong Siddeley cars, and many superb examples of other cars dating from 1920 to 1960 are on show. Part of this museum is dedicated to ex-bomber pilot and designer Ken Wallis. He was the pilot of the Wallis Autogyro flown by James Bond in the film 'You Only Live Twice'.

There is so much to see and do at Collectors World and no amount of reading about the place will prepare you for what your visit will show you. An old cobblers shop, a Charles Dickens Room where you will see characters and books together with experiencing the sounds and sights of Victorian England, and even a shrine to the Virgin Mary at Hermitage Hall. Want to know more? . . . an extensive antique and unusual dolls exhibition, horse drawn carts and carriages, farming memorabilia, etc. Must be seen.

BAROMETER WORLD
**Quicksilver Barn, Merton,
Okehampton, Devon
Tel: 01805 603443**

From rare and strange instruments from the past, to the bizarre natural weather forecasters such as frogs and leeches, you are certain to find Barometer World an exhibition full of amazement.

The barometer has always been the most important means of predicting weather changes. At Barometer World antique barometers are restored to their former glory, cases are repaired and repolished if needed, and fitments are cleaned or repaired either using authentic spares or parts made specially to suit.

The famous 'Leech Barometer' - also known as the 'Tempest Prognosticator' - was first exhibited by its inventor in 1851 at The Great Exhibition in London. It was a superb example of Victorian eccentricity being complex, gold plated, and used to predict storms using leeches! Barometer World has spent over 2 years researching and building a complete copy of it which can now be seen in their exhibition.

The workshop and museum will illustrate not only the importance of barometers but details the development of them from around 1600 to the present time. The weird and wonderful collection that can be seen here was started by retired bank manager Edwin Banfield in 1971. It contains banjo-shaped, mercury stick, and contra lube barometers, and even has a dolls house model. There are far too many to describe here but whether its a ships barometer or a thunder bottle barometer you are sure to find it here.

Apart from the incredible collection on

Barometers of all kinds can be seen at Barometer World - a day out with a difference.

display, Barometer World is the largest specialist firm dealing and restoring barometers in the world, and as such you may witness the amazing craftsmen skills in use. New and vintage barometers can be purchased here, and a small gift shop sells traditional and unusual barometer related items.

ROMANY MUSEUM
Clay Lake, Spalding,
Lincolnshire
Tel: 01775 710599

At the Romany Museum there is an amazing colourful collection of traditional horse-drawn Romany Vardoes (caravans) and carts. Learn about the Romany way of life, see the cooking utensils used over an open fire, or even venture into the fortune telling tent. The biggest collection of Romany photographs and sketches covering the last 150 years is kept here, and indeed this is the largest public display of Romany Vardoes and Romany history in the world.

For a Romany day out with a difference why not hire a horse-drawn Vardo here and enjoy a day in the countryside.

THE COLOUR MUSEUM
Providence Street, Bradford,
Yorkshire
Tel: 01274 390955

This is a museum dedicated to colour and is the only one of its kind in Europe. Interactive galleries and exhibitions demonstrate the weird and wonderful world of colour whilst explaining its development and technology. Situated in a former wool warehouse in the centre of Bradford, the museum has 2 main galleries called the World of Colour and Colour and Textiles - both absolutely packed with exciting things. Arranged along the different aspects of colour the exhibits are very much 'hands-on' and provide a wonderful opportunity for youngsters (and adults) to explore this fascinating subject. The second floor gallery explores all aspects of technological development, whilst workshops are regularly held here.

LAND OF LOST CONTENT
The Market Hall, Market Street,
Craven Arms, Shropshire
Tel: 01588 676176

Memories will come flooding back once you enter the Land of Lost Content. Set over 3 floors and featuring over 30 individual exhibit themes that are based on life during the 20th century, this was the result of sterling work by Stella Mitchell who collected and collated the items over many years with the assistance of her husband. Winkle-picker shoes, old teddies, food cartons, wirelesses, clothes, war memorabilia, and much, much more jostles for space with thousands and thousands of items that are guaranteed to make nostalgia kick in.

At the start of the exhibits area you will see what was eaten - when food really was food with no additives or preservatives. Music from an era long gone accompanies your journey through this huge collection of bygone objects, and information boards relay all you need to know about each era and the impact change has had. Many of us take for granted the numerous luxuries we have today such as computers, washing machines and colour televisions. A stroll through the Land of Lost Content will make you realise how truly lucky we are. Music legends, The Beatles, have a display here including albums, posters and instruments.

- what a gas -

GAS MUSEUM
**British Gas, Aylestone Road,
Leicester, Leicestershire
Tel: 0116 253 5506**

Opened in 1977, this is Britain's first specialist gas museum and is situated under a clock tower in the Victorian gatehouse of an actual gasworks in Leicester. It was established to preserve the knowledge of the industry when economic change arose and many of the artifacts on display here reflect that period when the conversion to natural gas took place. Following the demerger of British Gas in 1997, Transco and Centrica Plc set up a trust to take over the museum to preserve the items on display for the benefit of future generations. The collection has been described as 'the largest, most representative and significant holding of material related to the gas industry, its application and effects upon society, anywhere in the world'.

So what will you see here? The complete history of the industry for a start, in addition to the development of natural gas today. The use of gas for lighting in the 19th century, the all gas 1920's kitchen, and - believe it or not - a gas radio and gas hairdryer.

Milestones in the gas industry include the year 1684 when John Clayton managed to produce coal gas from the distillation of coal and stored it in bladders, and 1792 when William Murdoch illuminated his house in Cornwall by gas produced in an iron retort. In 1807 Pall Mall in London was first lit by gas from a centralised gasworks, and in 1817 Samuel Clegg installed a gasworks at the Royal Mint and developed an efficient gas meter.

There are many startling but true facts connected with gas. In 1858 the Washington USA Gas Company advised filling wet meters with whisky due to the fact that the more usual water froze during bad winters and cracked the meter.

In 1855 a newspaper article stated that the many children who were suffering whooping cough at the time should visit the gasworks to breathe the exhalations of the gas-lime.

Reverend John Clayton invited his guests to try an unusual party trick in 1684. The coal gas he had stored in pigskin bladders was to be lit by an invited guest pricking the bladder(s) and lighting the escaping gas to provide a gas light.

The 'Flamephone' was developed in 1922 by Jack Kitchen. This was a sound device that used gas burners to increase sound volume and produce amazing optical effects.

In Paris, around 1878, the New Opera House had 9,200 naked flame gas lights. The piping was controlled by 714 gas taps, and a chandelier had 556 burners eating up all the oxygen.

New Palace Yard, London, in 1868 was where the world's first traffic lights were installed. A revolving lantern was operated by a policeman with a lever and the rotating lantern showed a red or green light. This was very strange as the first motor car was yet to be invented.

BRAMAH TEA & COFFEE MUSEUM

**40 Southwark Street,
London SE1
Tel: 0207 403 5650**

For generations the London tea trade has blended, marketed and packaged tea, on both sides of the River Thames close to London Bridge. Tea auctions and many important warehouses connected with the industry were nearby and for 200 years the East India Company sailing ships that were returning from China would unload there.

The Bramah Tea & Coffee Museum is the world's first museum that is exclusively related to the history of tea and coffee. You can find out the 400 year old history of 2 of the world's most important commodoties here, and browse the ceramics, prints, samples and more, answering all your questions about these everyday drinks.

THE MUSEUM OF SMUGGLING HISTORY

**Botanic Gardens, Ventnor,
Isle of Wight
Tel: 01983 853677**

Over 700 years of smuggling history can be discovered at this most unusual underground museum located in a vault at the Botanic Gardens. Here you will learn the secrets of how contraband was moved from one area to another by smugglers and pirates, and find out all about smuggling through the ages.

Opened in 1973, this unique attraction has a deceptive frontage as the small building gives no idea of the actual size of the musem which contains over 300 exhibits in 3 big underground galleries. Gold, general contraband, and slaves were smuggled through ports, and this is the place to learn all about the smuggling rings and how they operated. Great fun for all the family.

WALSALL LEATHER MUSEUM
Littleton Street West, Walsall, West Midlands
Tel: 01922 721153

The sympathetically restored Victorian factory that now houses the Walsall Leather Museum tells the story about this interesting trade and how Walsall became the capital of Britain's leathergoods trade. Skilled craftsmen demonstrate their skills in authentic workshops and are always willing to stop and talk about their craft. Bags, wallets, bridles and saddles, together with a host of other leathergoods are exported all over the world from the dozens of companies still manufacturing in the town, and the shop at the museum offers a wide range of Walsall-made leathergoods at up to 50% off the recommended retail price.

Find out everything you want to know about the leather trade at the displays of past and present goods including unusual designer leatherwork.

HAT WORKS MUSEUM
Wellington Mill, Wellington Road South, Stockport, nr Manchester
Tel: 0845 8330975

This is the UK's first and only museum solely dedicated to hats and hat making. Exhibitions and special events take place throughout the year at the Hat Works and the stunning displays of hats manufactured over the centuries is quite spectacular. From fur hats of the early 1800's, to baseball caps, bowlers and top hats; in fact hats of every description, size and colour can be seen here.

Stockport has long had historic links with hatting and you can learn how the industry flourished - once employing almost 5,000 people by the end of the 19th century. Hat demonstrators reveal the art of hat making and you can see the 'planking kettle' where mercury was once used in the felting process. There is an extensive archive of historical photographs connected with the industry, and audio visual shows are really informative. You can even discover the origins of the phrase 'mad as a hatter'.

I can recall seeing Barney Rubble in an episode of The Flintstones with a dinosaur hat on his head. Wonder if its on display here?

At work on leather at the Walsall Leather Museum.

THE BAKELITE MUSEUM
Orchard Mill, Williton,
Somerset
Tel: 01984 632133

Quirky is what the page heading says, and there are thousands of quirky and rare items to be seen here including the Bakelite Coffin, huge perming machines, and even spy cameras. Bakelite is a hardened form of plastic and this museum boasts the largest collection of vintage plastics in the country. It showcases Art Deco styles from the 20th century, a fascinating display of Victorian plastics, and some of the strangest contraptions and things you are ever likely to see.

CHARNWOOD MUSEUM
Queens Hall, Granby Street,
Loughborough, Leicestershire
Tel: 01509 233754

Spot the 'Barrow Skipper' - this Jurassic marine reptile still 'swims' under the floor of the museum. Dig through layers of history and discover why archaeologists like old rubbish so much, or zoom in on a centipede's head with a video microscope. Crazy, but just a few of the mad things you can do at Charnwood Museum - a museum that cannot be edequately described or categorised by the writer. You can view ancient Anglo-Saxon treasures such as a gold sword pommel, look under rocks or in crevices to find the creatures that live in the museum, or investigate the 4,000 year old burial of 'Cossington Boy'. Try cranes, magnets, or enter the Victorian grocers shop. What a place.

AVONCROFT MUSEUM OF HISTORIC BUILDINGS
Stoke Heath, Bromsgrove,
Worcestershire
Tel: 01527 831363

This is a museum with a difference - it is an open-air museum of buildings. It may be the only museum of its kind in the world and it is certainly interesting. Craftsmen can be seen at work in a 19th century workshop and you can view revolutionary machinery that changed the face of architecture, but the main attractions here are the buildings. See Victorian Britain at the Toll House, Tudor life in the superb Merchants House, or a glimpse of life after World War II in the reconstructed Arcon V Prefab.

In all there are over 25 historic building exhibits plus traditional farm buildings such as a 19th century windmill. Structures include those made from brick, asbestos, fibreglass, concrete, and corrugated steel. The aims of the museum are to rescue, where possible, historic buildings from destruction, and to focus on a programme that tells visitors why these buildings are important and how they were used in the past. Bed and breakfast would be a good idea here.

3D WORLD
Quay Lane, Brading,
Isle of Wight
Tel: 07050 652061

A small museum worth mentioning for its holographs and psychedelic pictures.

THE SHERLOCK HOLMES MUSEUM
**221b Baker Street, London NW1
Tel: 0207 935 8866**

The creation of Sir Arthur Conan Doyle, Sherlock Holmes and Doctor Watson lived in a Victorian lodging house at 221b Baker Street between 1881 and 1904. Holmes, the super sleuth, is world famous as an enigmatic yet superb private detective whom Scotland Yard often called upon to assist their investigations into perpetrated crimes. The famous study overlooking Baker Street that has been seen in so many memorable films over the years is now part of a museum dedicated to his life and times. Here you can see his pipe, deerstalker hat, violin, and even his many disguises. Sit in his armchair to pose for a photograph, or enter his adjoining bedroom. All the rooms here contain personal belongings including Doctor Watson's second floor bedroom and the landlady Mrs Hudson's room.

Enigmatic, and the inspiration for so many books, films and plays, Holmes was a character sometimes shrouded in mystery. Visitors here frequently ask if he really lived at the house but alas, no actual records of the lodgers who lived during Victorian times exist.

Chemistry equipment, the diary of Doctor Watson, and much more can be seen at The Sherlock Holmes Museum. One of the most striking rooms here is the third floor exhibition room which has marvellous wax models that depict scenes from the stories. You can see Sherlock Holmes and Professor Moriaty (the arch villain who proved a thorn in Holmes's side on many occasions in the same room. A great selection of gifts including related memorabilia can be purchased in the ground floor souvenir shop of this excellent museum.

Were Holmes and Watson fictional characters, or did Sir Arthur Conan Doyle pen his stories based on fact? Local authority records do indicate that the house was indeed registered as a lodging house from the years 1860 to 1934, and state that some of the maids who worked at the premises were in fact related to a Mr Holmes. It is also known that a Doctor Watson lived next door in the period of the 1890's - although this Doctor Watson was an artificial teeth manufacturer. Perhaps we will never know. Methinks this is a case for Sherlock Holmes. Elementary my dear Watson.

FORGE MILL NEEDLE MUSEUM
**Needle Mill Lane, Riverside, Redditch, Worcestershire
Tel: 01527 62509**

Opened by the Queen in 1983, the Forge Mill Needle Museum tells the story of needle making during Victorian times and over the past 3 centuries. This is a step back in time as you soak in the atmosphere of a Victorian needle polishing mill which has some horrific tales to relate. The mill is a listed building and houses original water powered machinery, tools and work-benches used by workers. It illustrates not only how needles were made but also how Redditch came to be the master in the world needle trade.

The museum can be found next to the remains of Bordesley Abbey, a medieval Cistercian Abbey which has been extensively excavated.

- eccentric museums -

HORNIMAN MUSEUM
100 London Road, Forest Hill, London SE23. Tel: 0208 699 1872

Commissioned in 1898 and opened in 1901 the Horniman Museum is one of Britain's oddest museums. Frederick John Horniman - a millionaire as a result of his father's tea-importing business - was an avid collector of curiosities, following on from his father who himself was a proficient collector of artifacts. The Victorian age brought with it a rapid expansion in transport and communication and Frederick John Horniman set about enlightening the British public as to the wonders of the wider world.

Only a visit to the Horniman Museum will suffice as no amount of words can adequately describe the multitude of wonders you will see. There are 3 main collections; over 7,000 musical instruments with themes such as 'Rhythm of Life', Natural History which has over 250,000 specimens, and World Cultures (Ethnography) which has over 80,000 objects. All the collections are of national importance. One of the highlights is the aquarium which explores the interaction of humans and water. Tanks show startling species such as the 4-eyed fish from mangrove swamps and blind cave fish from Mexico. Collections here include masks, textiles, and amazing artifacts from all corners of the earth. The display case that runs the length of the stairs illustrates the progress of a river from its origins to its ending in a tidal estuary. There are Victorian examples of stuffed animals, a library collection, and even a replica of the Dodo.

This is one of Britain's most fascinating museums - to see so much of the world.

THACKRAY MUSEUM
Beckett Street, Leeds, Yorkshire. Tel: 0113 244 4343

Set in a former warehouse building adjacent to St.James Hospital, the vast museum collection here of over 35,000 surgical objects explains the ways people's lives have been improved as a result of increasing knowledge in medicine and healthcare over the last 150 or so years. There are many unique medical contraptions and devices to be seen including the bizarre metal 'Terminator' looking, 16th century orthopaedic correction frame. A huge range of surgical instruments dating from the 19th century to the present day includes some pretty spectacular examples of gruesome looking tools that were meant to assist the surgeon.

Also here is a collection of English pharmacy ceramics, and over 8,000 books including the largest collection of medical trade literature in the world. Thank goodness for modern 'quacks'.

Alaskan totem pole outside the Horniman Museum.

THE FAN MUSEUM
10 Crooms Hill, Greenwich, London SE10
Tel: 0208 305 1441

This is the only museum in the world completely dedicated to the ancient art and craft of fans and fan making. It houses the world's most important single collection of fans, fan leaves, and associated items in a pair of listed buildings - constructed in 1721 - which themselves are of great interest having been authentically restored to their original character and splendour.

Located in the heart of historic Greenwich, the museum also has an Orangery with a quite spectacular mural to admire. It overlooks a 'secret' garden in the Japanese manner and has a stream, pond, and oriental architectural features. This provides a haven of tranquility for visitors.

Since its opening in 1991 The Fan Museum has achieved awards from the National Art Collections Fund and the English Tourist Board, amongst others. Some of the delightful and intricate creations to be seen here will amaze. Fans may also be commissioned to your own individual design which would be ideal for a variety of functions and events such as weddings, product launches, corporate events, etc.

What is particulary interesting is the fact that this delightful place offers education and study facilities for all levels of interested parties - from primary school children right through to post-graduate researchers.

Visitors to The Fan Museum can enjoy viewing the designs of numerous unique fans and items which have seen use for many different purposes over many centuries. These include fashion accessories, symbolic use, ceremonial items, and commemorative presents. Altogether there are more than 3,500 mainly antique fans from all parts of the world to admire including many rare and exquisite examples. Fan-tastic.

THE CLINK PRISON MUSEUM
1 Clink Street, London SE1
Tel: 0207 403 6515

Located on the site of the original Clink Prison (probably the oldest prison in the country) this is the place where jailers were often merciless in their abuse of the prisoners. It possibly takes its name from either the old Dutch word 'klink' meaning gaol, or from the 'clinking' of chains. Either way this was the forerunner of today's expression for being in 'clink'.

In the shadows of London Bridge, this held prisoners from early Tudor times until 1780, with the majority of the inmates being prostitutes. In Tudor times particularly, affluent men from the City of London sought their pleasures with ladies of the night, predominantly in this part of London. At the museum you can find out about the horrors of torture that took place here, jailers who were easily bribed, and the many villains - some innocent and some guilty - who stepped into this place, including priests.

People commited to The Clink included petty thieves, murderers, and even those accused of practising the wrong faith. The hands-on torture devices show what hideous means were used to extract confessions from prisoners, and the gloomy surroundings here add to the atmosphere of your visit.

Part Two
- USA -

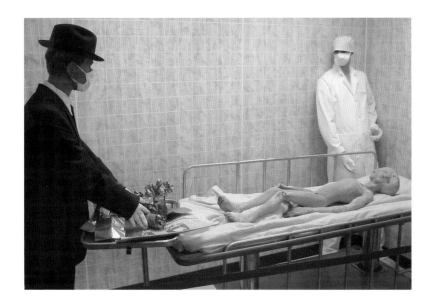

Greetings earthlings from the UFO Museum
in Roswell, New Mexico - page 50.

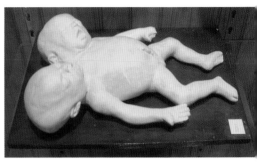

Step this way into the famous Mutter Museum at the College of Physicians of Philadelphia.

Amongst the most unusual sights you will ever behold is the giant 27ft long human colon, and the brains of murderers. See the conjoined twins (above right), the baby with 46 twists in the umbilical cord - the most ever recorded - (below left), and the little and large of the skeletal world (below right), where you can marvel at the skeletons of a giant and a midget.

MUTTER MUSEUM
19 South 22nd Street, Philadelphia, Pennsylvania

Where can you see the brains of murderers, skeletons of a giant and a midget, a gigantic 27ft long human colon, and a woman whose body deformed into soap? The Mutter Museum, which is found at the College of Physicians of Philadelphia, is a place of incredible sights that will live in the memory long after you have had a privileged view into this strange world. It was mostly frequented during its early days by visiting physicians and medical students, but today the general public represent the majority of visitors who come to learn and marvel at the massive collection of medical monstrosities that is assembled here.

The museum's collections include over 20,000 objects comprising anatomical and pathological specimens and including over 900 fluid preserved specimens, medical instruments, pathalogical models, and assorted memorabilia that will truly astound you. The remarkable collections of Dr. Mutter which are housed here date back in part to approximately 1863 when the museum was first opened in a different location. Although greatly added to since, some of the original items remain the most striking.

The strangest things you will ever see includes the brains of animals - from a small frog to a man - and very often with eyes attached. Other brains on display are those of epileptics, the grey matter of hanged murderer John Wilson (and other murderers), and various slices of heads that include brain. A large collection of deformed babies, skull collections with holes cut in them, models of skin diseases, bones showing the ravages of syphilis, and a display of eyeballs with assorted injuries in the Eye Wall of Shame - including one with a toothpick jutting out of the retina - are just a few of the sights that will shock.

The upper balcony shows a history of conjoined twins including the case of 'Chang and Eng' - with the genuine liver attached! Also in this section is a gangrenous hand, a woman with a deformed ribcage caused by a lifetime of wearing a corset, and the remarkable 'Soap Lady' - a woman who died of Yellow Fever and was buried in soil that had chemical properties which turned her into soap. An Iron Lung can be seen in the polio exhibit, and Legionnaire's Disease, the hearing organs of mammals, and even a freeze-dried cat get space here.

For those of us who often complain of wind or feeling bloated, spare a thought for the poor soul who was diagnosed with a gross enlargement of the colon in days before x-rays. This 27ft long python-like organ can be seen in all its glory in a glass display case. Another exhibit here is dedicated to infectious diseases, a collection of long forgotten medicines and gruesome medical devices can be seen, and even Abraham Lincoln's bloodstained collar is displayed. Quite harrowing is the collection that documents various deformaties that can occur on the skeleton. It includes the case of 30 year old Harry Eastlack whose disease - fibrodysplasia ossificans progressiva - caused his bones to become almost like concrete.

For curiosity value the best collection here has to be the Chevalier Jackson Collection of over 2,000 objects that have been swallowed and removed from the human body. Drawers are marked 'seeds', 'coins', 'nuts', 'shells', and even 'bones' and 'dental material'. Can people really swallow their dentures?

LEILA'S HAIR MUSEUM
**1333 South Noland Road,
Independence, Missouri**

Over 2,000 pieces of jewellery and almost 200 wreaths on display here have one thing in common - they are all made from or contain human hair. All made prior to 1900, this is possibly the only hair museum in the world and it has featured in numerous magazines and newspaper articles and on television entertainment programmes. Leila Cohoon who founded the museum began collecting hair as a hobby over 40 years ago.

The numerous hair wreaths on display, some in original frames, were considered pieces of art, and unusual examples include a couple of wreaths from sisters whose heads were shaved before they started life in a convent, and a family history book dating from 1725 to 1900 made with samples of each of the family member's hair. Another strange exhibit is a 'hair tree' made from the hair of several members of one family.

The museum has earrings, buttons, brooches, necklaces, watch straps, and all manner of other human ornamentation, each made from or containing human hair. The collection is constantly being added to although preserving the old pieces is a full-time job in itself.

Leila's Hair Museum is the national headquarters for the Victorian Hairwork Society, an organization who hold annual 'Hairball' conventions that they claim to be great successes. Their mission statement is as follows - 'To provide an organization to bring people together - people who are interested in the art of hair work. To create an atmosphere for promoting and learning about the art. To promote and provide accurate information about the history, heritage, preservation, restoration, and continuation of all types of hair work so that it can be elevated to its rightful place as a folk art'. Pretty hairy stuff don't you think. My local barber is the only one who's getting his hands on my hair.

DOG MUSHING MUSEUM
**250 Cushman Street,
Courthouse Square,
Fairbanks, Alaska**

This is said to be the most comprehensive dog mushing exhibition in the world. Dog mushing (or dog sledding as it is more commonly known) is Alaska's state sport and during earlier times it was a vital means of transport when winters were harsh. The museum features exhibits of various types of dog sleds including racing sleds, mushing equipment and memorabilia, harnesses, trophies, and even a theatre showing mushing videos. A multi-media library includes back issues of Mushing Magazine for the more avid enthusiast.

Housed in Fairbanks historic City Hall, the museum opened in 1987 and gets plenty of local and casual visitors. Not a place for cat lovers.

NEW ORLEANS HISTORIC VOODOO MUSEUM
724 Dumaine Street, New Orleans, Louisiana

Voodoo, the Haitian folk religion that consists of African magical beliefs and rites fused with certain Catholic elements, is a spellbinding subject that even today still has the power to strike fear into the hearts of its believers. Marie Leaveau was probably the most famous practitioner of Voodoo and she reigned supreme as the Voodoo Queen of New Orleans throughout most of the 19th century until her death in 1881, aged 98.

This museum provides a genuine insight into the mystery of Voodoo with items on display including portraits, 'Gris-Gris' (bags filled with charms, bones and herbs), potions, Voodoo dolls, African artifacts that influenced the growth of the religion, and even Marie Leaveau's magical 'wishing stump' which is said to bestow good fortune on those who touch it. The art of Voodoo is still widely practised in New Orleans and this is an informative - if somewhat spooky - guide to all aspects of it. Incidentally, New Orleans is believed to be America's most haunted city.

Further reading: see 'New Orleans Cemetery & Gris-Gris Walking Tour' featured in Strangest Tours in Britain. Details on how to order see page 96.

LUNCHBOX MUSEUM
River Market Antiques, 3226 Hamilton Road, Colombus, Georgia

Allen Woodall began collecting lunch boxes because, as he puts it, "they're just so neat". The American lunch box was always a big thing, much more so in the USA than in Britain - or anywhere else in the world for that matter. Allen's museum is as unusual as its location; above a country music radio station in Columbus (which he also owns), and it boasts more than 1,000 lunch boxes in addition to related memorabilia such as coolers, thermos flasks, and even tobacco tins which were used as lunch boxes.

Pop culture is in abundance here with lunch boxes adorned with 'Charlies Angels', 'Flipper' the famous dolphin, and the one-time idols of millions of young girls - the Osmond brothers. The passion of the collector is in much evidence here and there are some superb artistic examples in the collection. Although plastic is the most widely used material today (as metal lunch boxes were deemed 'lethal weapons' by Florida Legislature in 1986), the vintage collection of metal boxes are the most striking.

Whether your box was metal or plastic, and had a teen idol, cartoon character, or even a personalised lid, the chances are you will see a similar one on show here. Evoke those childhood memories with a visit to this entertaining museum.

JELL-O MUSEUM
23 E.Main Street, LeRoy, New York

In Britain its simply called Jelly, but in America it goes by the name of Jell-O; yes its our wobbly gelatin friend made in delicious flavours such as strawberry, orange and lemon, that millions of kids love.

In 1845, Peter Cooper patented a product which was 'set' with gelatin, although it never took off with the American public at that time. Then, in 1897, Pearle Wait was concocting a cough remedy and laxative in his home in LeRoy. He experimented with gelatine and somehow came up with a fruit flavoured dessert which his wife, May, named Jell-O. Lack of capital and marketing experience restricted sales and the secret formula was thus sold in 1899 for $450 to a neighbour who was a medicine manufacturer. It was then subsequently sold on again and, in 1900, the Jell-O name was first used by the Genesee Pure Food Company. Their advertising campaign was so successful that in 1902 Jell-O sales amounted to $250,000. In 1909 it was over $1 million, and 4 years later it was double that. The rest is history. Jell-O was exported all over the world from 1964, and today, Jell-O is manufactured by Kraft/General Foods in Dover, Delaware.

Find out all about the remarkable history of Jell-O at the Jell-O museum. Reservations are said to be encouraged (heaven knows why as a stampede to a jelly emporium is mind-boggling), and yes, the obligatory gift shop can be found on the premises.

Brisbane, Australia, in 1981, saw George Ross and Paul Squires create the world's largest Jell-O. It was set in a tank and consisted of 7,700 gallons ($14,000 worth) of pink Jell-O, and was entered in the Guiness Book of Records.

It is said that the people of Salt Lake City get through more lime flavoured Jell-O than any other city in America.

Hospital technicians tested a bowl of Jell-O with an EEG machine in 1993 and confirmed an earlier testing that found Jell-O has brain waves identical to adult people.

- does my bomb look big in this -

TITAN MISSILE MUSEUM
1580 W.Duval Mine Road, Green Valley, Arizona

There were 18 Titan missile silos that once surrounded Tucson, Arizona. They were de-activated as a result of the SALT Treaty, but one was retained for public viewing - perhaps as a grim reminder of what might have been. Your visit to the command centre here, which incorporates the museum, will amaze you. The complex is mounted on springs and can withstand anything except a direct hit. The 6,000 pound blast doors you walk through take you to the silo itself - 100ft below ground. The awesome looking missile is over 100ft tall, and although empty and de-activated now, it weighed 170 tons when fully fueled and ready to take off. A huge sliding door that once protected the missile is now sealed halfway open, and a 2ft hole has been cut in the re-entry vehicle nosecone so that Russian 'spy' satellites can tell the missile is de-activated.

With your hard-hat still on you proceed to the War Room where directions for the proposed missile target, perhaps 7,000 miles away, would have been fed into the guidance system. Launch keys and secret codes are kept here and 2 different keys would have had to be inserted into different parts of the computer system to activate the missile. That would have been the point of no return as different lights and alarms came on, then silence. Meanwhile, on the other side of the world, people would have been unaware that a 170 ton metal bird with a destructive power that beggars belief was hurtling towards them with an unwanted nest-egg.

NATIONAL LIGHTER MUSEUM
Sooner Road, Guthrie, Oklahoma

Zippos, Ronsons, table models, and examples from both World Wars - in fact there are thousands of lighters on display here including some that are hundreds of years old. This is the only museum of its kind in the world and it was established to gather information on lighters and the manufacture of lighters. The museum relies solely on donations from lighter enthusiasts and collectors from around the world and has about 30,000 pieces on display including numerous fire starters.

When tobacco was first introduced it soon became popular throughout the world. With it came hundreds of styles of lighters and it is estimated that there are now multi-millions of standard and innovative lighters - such as those presented as long company service awards - waiting to be discovered in bottom drawers everywhere. When a lighter has a name, date, or event engraved on it, it becomes a historic document. Have you got a light boy?

NATIONAL ATOMIC MUSEUM
Kirtland Air Force Base, Wyoming

The National Atomic Museum is operated by the Department of Energy (DOE) and contains a large collection of declassified nuclear technology. Its objective is to provide a repository of educational materials connected with the subject, and provide information on the Atomic Age.

Located around the outside of the museum are many large exhibits including the Boeing B-52B jet bomber that dropped the United States last air burst H-bomb in 1962, and a 280mm Atomic cannon that was once America's most powerful field artillery.

The 'Low Bay' area of the museum is devoted to exhibits based on the research and development of various forms of nuclear energy, whilst the 'High Bay' section features the story of the unprecedented 2.2 billion dollar 'Manhattan Project' that was centred in New Mexico during World War II. This was the project that developed, built, and tested the world's first Atomic bomb. Highly interesting, if a little scary.

THE KANSAS BARBED WIRE MUSEUM
120 West 1st Street, LaCrosse, Kansas

In 1874, Joseph Glidden designed a particular kind of wire fencing which he then patented and named barbed wire. With the slogan 'Cheaper than dirt and stronger than steel', it mushroomed into a multi-million dollar industry and changed the face of the West forever. Over the years it has been utilised for a multitude of uses including dividing sections of prairie for the restraint of cattle, and as a means of defence in the military conflicts of every war.

LaCrosse is home to the annual Kansas Barbed Wire Collectors Association (KBWCA) Swap and Sell - which is held each May. This annual festival attracts barbed wire enthusiasts from all parts of the country and includes a barbed wire splicing contest.

The Kansas Barbed Wire Museum itself has an astonishing range of collectibles on display including over 2,000 barbed wire varieties, antique fencing tools, and a display of military wire and wire tools. There are also some bizarre exhibits to be seen such as a massive, authentic Ravens nest built out of barbed wire. It was discovered in Greeley County, Kansas, in the 1960's. Samples of barbed wire that was manufactured between 1870 and 1890 can be seen, and the museum illustrates the midwest's important contributions to America's past. The Barbed Wire Hall of Fame gets right to the point and tells you all you need to know at the sharp end of barbed wire.

DEVIL'S ROPE MUSEUM
100 Kingsley Street, McLean, Texas

Another place that is dedicated to barbed wire is the Devil's Rope Museum (history often refers to barbed wire as the "Devil's Rope"). Set in good ol' Texas on famous Route 66 this proclaims itself to be the largest barbed wire historic museum in the world; a fact which one would imagine would be disputed by The Kansas Barbed Wire Museum. If you happen to be in the vicinity of the Texas Panhandle with nothing better to do why not call in here to admire barbed wire samples, barbed wire artifacts, barbed wire memorabilia, and the history of barbed wire. The museum has an unmistakable frontage; 2 gigantic balls of barbed wire perched on 2 columns.

Believe it or not barbed wire collecting is a popular hobby in America and the Devil's Rope Museum offers an appraisal service to collectors for insurance purposes.

The Devil's Rope Museum located in Texas on Route 66 and (below) one of the more unusual exhibits - a hat made of barbed wire.

BARNEY SMITH'S TOILET SEAT ART MUSEUM
239 Abiso Avenue, Alamo Heights, Texas

Many of Barney Smith's toilet seats were made using materials that were donated to him. People mail him with something unique, and in some instances it ends up preserved forever on a seat, lid or throne - whichever you wish to call it. Barney has been creating these works of art for over 30 years and there are now well over 700 decorated toilet seats in his collection.

Barney was a master plumber before retirement, and his unusual hobby started when he needed a place to mount a set of small deer antlers. His toilet seat lid was roughly the right shape so he stuck the antlers on the lid, and so it all began. Every seat in the collection is numbered and photographed, with documentation about the materials used and the inspiration for each particular work. All of the seats are the pressed wood variety (sawdust and glue) as the solid wood type are too striking in colour, whilst plastic lids can't be painted and carved precisely. A local company donates all the seats and there are always many 'blanks' in the workshop waiting to be transformed following a flash of inspiration.

Perhaps the most unusual seat in the collection is the one containing a genuine marijuana leaf. The back of the seat has been signed by the Chief of San Antonio Police allowing it to be displayed for 'educational purposes'.

THE AMERICAN SANITARY PLUMBING MUSEUM
39 Piedmont Street, Worcester, Massachusetts

We have flushed out the strangest museum in Massachusetts - The American Sanitary Plumbing Museum in Worcester. It was founded by plumbing equipment distributor Charles Manoog in 1979 and is said to be the only known plumbing museum in the world.

Ornate porcelain toilets, an 'earth cabinet' that collected your droppings in lime instead of water, and chain-pull toilets with high wooden tanks are all on show here. You can also find out about, and see, the evolution of toilet paper including samples from the 1800's when it was referred to as 'boudoir paper'. Some very bizarre things were used to wipe the butt in years past. Add to the above hundreds of different fittings, pipes, and general memorabilia, and you can see why this peculiar shrine to the history of plumbing attracts so many visitors.

The American Sanitary Plumbing Museum is certainly a day out with a difference and, unexpectedly, quite interesting. No need to ask the way to the toilets here as you can find them everywhere.

SALEM WITCH MUSEUM
**Washington Square North,
Salem, Massachusetts**

Scary, memorable, and thought provoking - the Salem Witch Museum is all of these, and more. The main theme of the museum is the story and audio-visual presentation of the notorious witchcraft trials which took place in Salem during early spring in 1692. By the summer of that year many hundreds of people had been accused and imprisoned, victims of a society that was riddled with superstition and fear. The court that was formed to try the victims meted out harsh and quick sentences. One victim was crushed to death by rocks being loaded onto his chest, and dozens of others were hanged during a summer of executions.

Life-sized figures, eerie lighting, and compelling narration give a vivid overview of these infamous trials, and other exhibits trace the history of witches, witchcraft, and the drama of witch hunts. Not for the faint hearted. Incidentally, the museum is situated in a former church.

*There's no mistaking the signs at the famous Salem Witch Museum.
Exhibits include a reconstruction of the notorious witch trials of 1692.*

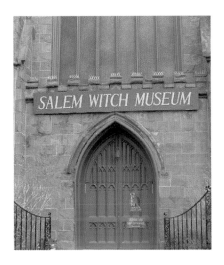 

- alien autopsy -

Tongue-in-cheek dummies or a representation of the real thing at the International UFO Museum & Research Centre.

INTERNATIONAL UFO MUSEUM & RESEARCH CENTRE
114 N.Main Street, Roswell, New Mexico

Meet the bug-eyed little men and find out all you need to know about alleged landings, hoax theories, and a whole lot more to do with our extraterrestrial friends. Opened in 1991, the International UFO Museum & Research Centre has welcomed hundreds of thousands of curious visitors since then and with the implementation of interactive technologies in the museum it has now become the main source of information relating to UFO's and the mystery surrounding them.

This entertaining place is dedicated to the most famous alleged crash landing site of a UFO, which occurred on ranchland some 70 miles from the small town of Roswell in New Mexico. It is said that the strange materials recovered from the debris were unlike anything ever seen before, having most unusual properties, and a military cover-up is said by many to be the reason that the world is none the wiser since the dramatic event took place - despite much speculation and research since. Newspaper reports from all over the USA reported on the event and cuttings from many of these can be seen at the museum. There is also a recreated scene of the Alien Autopsy hoax.

There is a huge amount of thought - provoking material to be seen here including some impressive photographs which seem to lend substance to the idea that we are not alone. Maps of alleged crash sites, a comprehensive library, and hundreds of alien themed items certainly make you stop and think as you browse this quaint yet modern museum.

Visitors here are actively encouraged to put forward their own speculations, theories or experiences, and you can even book here to have a tour of the famous crash site if you wish.

THE SKYSCRAPER MUSEUM
39 Battery Place, New York City, New York

Founded in 1996, the Skyscraper Museum is an educational corporation devoted to the study of high-rise buildings, past, present, and future. You can find it in New York City, the world's first vertical metropolis, and wander through the many exhibitions that explore tall buildings as objects of design and products of technology. The museum also celebrates New York City's rich architectural heritage and the many individuals who have helped shape its successive skylines.

This is a high-tech place to visit with many current and future exhibitions and projects taking place. They also offer 'Cool Stuff for Kids'.

THE CONSPIRACY MUSEUM
110 S.Market Street, Dallas, Texas

At the gift shop here you can purchase a pre-1963 salt shaker of JF Kennedy in a rocking chair, in which the salt pours out of a hole in the back of his head. Think that's bizarre? The latest addition here is that a security guard's gun killed JFK, and the assassin's shot missed. For $250 - as a contribution towards ballistic tests - you will receive a bullet, shell, and letter of authenticity!

The museum embraces all aspects of conspiracy, and all things conspiratorial, then strings them together. It was funded by a retired architect who calls himself an 'assassinologist' and expands on the public's skepticism about the Kennedy assassination, and the government in general. Mind-boggling.

All things bizarre can be seen at the Belhaven Memorial Museum such as the pig born with 2 snouts, and numerous specimen jars whose preserved contents often defy belief.

BELHAVEN MEMORIAL MUSEUM
210 E.Main Street, Belhaven, North Carolina

This remarkable non-profit making museum, run on a shoestring budget and with no air conditioning, holds the collections of Mrs Eva Blount Way, a peculiar woman and avid collector who simply couldn't throw anything away. She died in 1962 at the age of 92 and everything in her home was moved to the museum 3 years later. Her sprawling house, probably still empty now, has deterred prospective buyers who are perhaps wary of what they may discover. When you read of the contents of the Belhaven Memorial Museum you will understand why.

Eva Blount Way's hoarding began with a small collection of buttons given to her by her mother-in-law. Over the years she amassed over 30,000 more buttons from all over the world. She also began acquiring all manner of other items and, as word of her preoccupation spread, friends and neighbours began to bring their own gifts from their own lives and travels. The result is quite astonishing. The museum, which "collects, displays and preserves, historical and cultural artifacts and objects to encourage interest and support of the history, art, science and culture of the Belhaven area", has devoted the whole of the second floor of the museum to the eclectic collections of Mrs Eva Blount Way.

The majority of the collection was gathered in the early 1900's as a means of raising money for the American Red Cross and includes an 8-legged pig, a pig born with 2 snouts, a wedding party of dressed fleas, and 3 freak prenatal babies in specimen jars (which were given to Mrs Way by the town doctor). Jars of Mrs Way's home canned products, including chicken fat, jostle for space with an unspent Civil War Shell, a German World War I half-boot (which could have been amputated along with the foot), and a dress worn by a 700lb local woman who died in bed and had to be hoisted out of the bedroom window.

There are far too many peculiarities and monstrosities to be listed here, and most defy belief. A single eyed fetal pig, a 2-headed kitten, mummified squirrels, huge pickled tumours retrieved from the local hospital, and horrible looking cataracts and ingrown toenails all find their place here.

This fascinating array of artifacts from Beaufort County includes many items from Mrs Way's natural environment, everyday things such as dolls, toys, farm tools and clothing. But it is the specimen jars that arouse the most interest and draw the biggest gasps from visitors. Many have labels describing the contents, but who knows what some of them contain.

Such a strange museum is the Belhaven Memorial Museum. Where else would you see a collection of 30,000+ buttons alongside several snakes (killed by Mrs Way), one of which is stuffed, another made into a necktie, and a further one swallowing a wooden egg.

If seeing what a hare-lipped dog looks like is your idea of entertainment then the Belhaven Memorial Museum is the place for you. The museum builds upon the collections of Mrs Eva Blount Way and certainly breaks new ground in the world of the weird.

The American Visionary Art Museum has over 4,000 pieces in its collection, most of which are quite bizarre. The male figure (above left) is made entirely out of telephone wire, whilst the giant metallic 'faberge' type egg (above right) stands outside the main building. The gift shop has numerous handcrafted gifts, and many that will bring a smile to your face - including those shown below.

AMERICAN VISIONARY ART MUSEUM
800 Key Highway, Baltimore, Maryland

Over 4,000 pieces constitute the permanent collection at the American Visionary Art Museum although the museum states it is "committed to unveiling a great range of the best of visionary art by exploring one unifying theme at a time". As such there are constantly changing displays and they showcase some quite amazing works.

So what is Visionary Art? As defined by the museum's Mission Statement it is "art produced by self-taught individuals, usually without formal training, whose works arise from an innate personal vision that revels foremost in the creative act itself". Or in short, they state: "visionary art begins by listening to the inner voices of the soul, and often may not even be thought of as 'art' by its creator". I'm none the wiser, are you?

Anyway, what do you see at the museum? Well, first and foremost, the main building has been critically acclaimed as an 'architectural jewel', comprising 35,000 sq.ft and containing numerous galleries. Exhibits worth mentioning here are the car covered with 5,000 psychically bent forks and spoons produced by notable psychic Uri Geller, a 10ft model of the ship Lusitania made completely out of matchsticks, the world's largest ball of bras, and a man made entirely out of telephone wire. Some, or all of the above, may have been temporary exhibits as the museum has a fast turnaround of artists work.

What is permanent is The Whirligig, a 55ft tall wind powered, pinwheel-like sculpture made from car parts, bicycle wheels and cables. It stands in Sculpture

Plaza as a symbol of the museum's mission. Apart from the main building and Sculpture Plaza there is also the Tall Sculpture Barn which has 45ft high ceilings and can accommodate towering exhibits. This once housed a life-size, interactive chess set of sculpted metal angels and aliens.

Other sections of the American Visionary Art Museum include the Wildflower Garden, and a wedding chapel and altar built entirely out of tree limbs and flowers. The obligatory museum shop is one of the best you will find. Visitors looking for unusual gift ideas will find a whole host of international crafts, exotic charms, and weird and wonderful items for sale here.

Making sense of what you see at the American Visionary Art Museum is not easy. Andy Warhol's work seemed sane by comparison. It is however a day out with a difference and certainly thought provoking.

- listen, do you want to know a secret -

Codemakers and codebreakers at the National Cryptologic Museum.

NATIONAL CRYPTOLOGIC MUSEUM
Ft.George G, Meade, Maryland

The National Cryptologic Museum shares America's cryptologic legacy with the nation and is the National Security Agency's principal gateway to the public. Codemakers and codebreakers have been vital here for over 50 years and it is now seen as very important that information is shared with the public to educate it on the Agency's mission to protect the nation. How much you see is still down to faceless bureaucrats.

Open since 1993, the National Cryptologic Museum has around 50,000 visitors a year from around the world and provides an insight into the secretive world of codes and ciphers. The museum contains thousands of artifacts that illustrate the history of the cryptologic profession and you can catch a glimpse into the lives of the people who devoted their entire life into the defence of the nation by the machines, devices, and techniques they developed.

Exhibits here include Cold War Aerial Reconnaissance, Supercomputers, Biometrics, Women in American Cryptology, and the Vietnam War. They also have a rare book collection, old artifacts from the American Civil War such as the Union Code Book and Confederate Cipher Cylinder, and World War II Code Talkers and Enigma. If this is all too highbrow for you then go and see the reconnaissance aircraft at the adjacent National Vigilance Park.

MUSEUM OF CREATION & EARTH HISTORY
10946 Woodside Avenue, North Santee, California

Find the answers to those all important questions at the Museum of Creation & Earth History such as - Where did I come from? What is the meaning of life?

The museum is 4,000 sq.ft broken up into a series of rooms and hallways. It chronicles the events from the dawn of Creation up to the present day starting off with the Acts of God, Day 1 - the birth of the Universe. Each section is numbered by the day it occurred, and according to the Book of Genesis.

Death and Decay is an exhibit of animal and human skulls illustrating the inevitable order of things in the physical world, whilst Universal Disorder can be quite disturbing with sound effects that include babies crying and animal noises.

Other rooms have bizarre themes such as the Tower of Babel Room which has occult spiritism and astrological elements, and the room with framed portraits from the 18th and 19th centuries of prominent figures who believed in the biblical explanation of things.

The Ice Age Room is decorated with blue icicles, whilst the Evolutionary Tree is a twisted treetrunk with no leaves but bearing the fruit of 'Harmful Philosophies' and 'Evil Practices' which include promiscuity, bestiality, drugs, and genocide. All very strange.

Noah's Ark and the Great Flood, God in his great wisdom, and the Mt. St.Helens eruption of 1980 all play a part here as do many other characters and events. Meant to be linked in some manner, this mish-mash collection of colourful exhibits will blur your worldly vision, but it apparently gets visitors nevertheless.

NATIONAL MUSEUM OF FUNERAL HISTORY
415 Barren Springs Drive, Houston, Texas

Could death ever be so funny? This was opened in 1992 by Robert L.Waltrip, following 25 years of dreaming of an institute that would educate the public and preserve the heritage of the funeral industry. The museum states its purpose is to honour "one of our most important cultural rituals", but looking at the range of 'Fantasy Coffins' that are a speciality here at the workshops, your burial would be anything but dignified. The collection is apparently the largest assemblage of fantasy coffins outside of Ghana. What an accolade, but it seems Ghanian culture states that "life is a march towards the grave" and these coffins are believed to protect the well-being of the deceased in the after-world.

Coffins on show include a Mercedes Benz, a fish, a chicken, a crab, a shallot, and - believe it or not - even a Yamaha outboard motor. All hand crafted and ready for occupation, the coffins are said to symbolise different things. For example the leopard coffin is said to signify a person with power.

There is also much to do with funerals, and death in general to be seen at the museum including hearses, a 1916 Packard funeral bus that could carry the coffin, pallbearers, and 20 mourners (to eliminate funeral processions), embalming stuff, and a 'Funerals of the Famous' gallery. Not to be missed is the solid glass coffin, and the 'casket for 3'.

Great stuff in the gift shop such as a coffin golf putter, casket shaped candy bars, and a video entitled The History of Embalming. The NMFH even sponsors a Golf Classic. Spooky, but dead funny.

MUSEUM OF QUESTIONABLE MEDICAL DEVICES

Science Museum of Minnesota, 120 West Kellogg Boulevard, Saint Paul, Minnesota

Bob McCoy, international expert on medical quackery, was the proprietor/curator of the Museum of Questionable Devices when it was situated in downtown Minneapolis. He entertained visitors with some of his fantastic machines such as the 'Timely Warning Device' which was a barbed metal ring that sufferers of nocturnal emissions could wear on their penises to prevent an unwanted occurrence taking place, or the 'Skull-Reading Device' on one of the phrenology machines which would often raise a few giggles. These days the little museum has long since closed and Bob has retired, but the majority of his collection can still be seen at the Science Museum of Minnesota in Saint Paul.

The collections gallery has a phrenology machine that 'deduced' your personality, the 'Allure Bust Development Device', and a 1950's 'Shoe Fitting X-Ray Device' that claimed a perfect shoe fit every time. One of the more bizarre devices is the 'Ruth Drown Radio Therapy Machine' which analyses saliva and emits healing rays. She managed to get thousands of gullible people to subscribe to it in the 1960's.

Another incredulous contraption is the ''MacGregor Rejuvenator''. This was invented by a man from Seattle in the 1930's who claimed it could reverse the aging process. The patient was bombarded with magnetic fields, radio waves, and ultraviolet. The inventor obviously forgot to rejuvenate himself as we don't see any MacGregor Rejuvenator's on sale in my part of the world.

You can see an entire range of machines and contraptions on show here dating from 1790 to the present time, and they claim to do everything from straightening your nose to stimulating the 'abdominal brain'. There is even an 'Ultraviolet Comb' complete with penile and anal attachments. Unbelievably, quackery devices and gadgets are still sold to gullible people today. Some mighty strange patents get registered.

The Science Museum of Minnesota has a lot more to offer that just the Museum of Questionable Medical Devices. The Egyptian Mummy, 7ft diameter Douglas-fir tree trunk, Emily the 2-headed turtle, and numerous fossils and minerals are a few that spring to mind. Skulls and bones, sand from around the world, and almost 2 million objects in their collections all make for an exciting day out.

Collectors Corner is where children can get involved. They can bring 2 natural objects in that they have discovered such as skulls, shells, etc. They receive points for what they know about their discovery, which can subsequently be traded for other things or specimens - even at a later date.

Great fun here for all the family so wotcha waiting for.

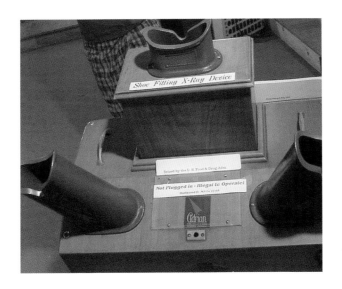

Amongst the many astonishing old medical contraptions and machines at the Museum of Questionable Medical Devices is the Shoe Fitting X-Ray Device (above), and (below) the Allure Bust Development Device from the 1950's.

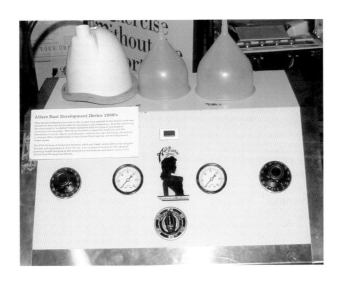

MISTER ED'S ELEPHANT MUSEUM
6019 Chambersburg Road, Orrtanna, Pennsylvania

Mister Ed's Elephant Museum has one of the largest and most unique collections of elephants in the world. Ed Gotwalt has elephants on the brain, so his visitors tell him. He first started collecting them in 1967 when he received his first one as a good luck gift on his wedding day. His collection grew to such a huge size that his wife made him open a museum to house them all and his collection now numbers over 6,000 elephant-related pieces including an elephant potty chair, an elephant shaped hair dryer, and even an elephant pulling a 24-carat gold circus truck.

The elephants and related pieces at Mister Ed's Elephant Museum are made from almost every substance known to man, and the collection has been compiled from all corners of the world. The bulk of the displays are housed in 2 long rooms with items both large and very tiny - the tiny items being displayed on narrow glass shelves. Many are serious collectors items and quite valuable.

The gift shop has a large range of associated big-eared memorabilia, and quite striking is the almost 10ft tall white elephant out in the road, presumably to attract passers-by. It has animated eyes and ears, and its voice is triggered by a hidden electric eye. Going by the name of Miss Ellie, it is a major attraction for children. The number of visitors here means Mr Ed is certainly no dumbo.

BUCKHORN SALOON & MUSEUM

318 East Houston Street, San Antonio, Texas

This is actually 5 museums for the price of one. The curiosity filled freak show that is the Buckhorn Museum has oddities such as the 8-legged lamb with 3 ears, a giant Woolly Mammoth head made of steel wool mounted on a plaque, and a cathedral made of 50,000 wooden matchsticks.

Originally opened in downtown San Antonio in 1881, owners Albert and Emile Friedrich, in true pioneering spirit, promised customers they could bring in their deer antlers and trade them for a shot or 2 of whiskey.The Buckhorn's collection of antlers, animals and oddities, subsequently grew. The Buckhorn Bar has many original furnishings, and the sprawling 2-storey museum contains some of the most unusual exhibits you will see anywhere. Jam-packed everywhere are things such as miniature saddles, over 8ft wide horns from 'Old Tex', the longest Texas Longhorn, the famous movie horse 'Calico' mounted in an alcove near a stairway, and everything else from 2-headed calves to albino creatures.

The Hall of Horns boasts more than 1,200 trophy mounts including an imposing African gorilla. Are they all real? This place has to be seen to be believed as its a never ending journey into gratuitous taxidermy and downright wackiness. Rare fish and birds galore at The Hall of Fins and Feathers including a 1,056 pound marlin - a world record. The Hall of Texas History Wax Museum here has a reproduction of a Commanche Indian scalping a settler - while his wife and child await their turns. Charming.

THE GHOSTS OF DEADWOOD GULCH WAX MUSEUM

12 Lee Street, Deadwood, South Dakota

The Ghosts of Deadwood Gulch Wax Museum features an audio-visual presentation of the great moments in Western History. Over 50 wax figures depict 19 moments from when Dakota was a territory and not a state. Some scenes are visually stunning, accompanied by dramatic lighting and sound effects, whilst others are representative of the boring daily activities of a frontier town.

Rowdy Dance Hall, Discovery of Gold, and Saloon Poker Game are 3 of the most impressive reproductions. The Poker Game is where the said coward Jack McCall crept up and shot famous gunslinger Wild Bill Hickok in the back of the head. Hickok had only arrived in Deadwood a few weeks previously. It is said that he had never once in his life sat with his back to a door - until that day. Also to be seen in this saloon scene is the Death Chair of Wild Bill Hickok, in an alcove above the front door in a glass case. A re-enactment of that fatal poker game occurs several times a day for the benefit of tourists. There is no way of knowing if some of the memorabilia on show here is genuine or not. Plenty of other places with lucrative tourist-cash related aspirations claim to have the 'genuine article'. Seems like another attraction thats rolled off the tourist-trap treadmill. Living on memories - its a hard habit to break.

Interestingly, on a ridge above the town, you can visit the final resting place of both Wild Bill Hickok and Calamity Jane in Mt. Moriah Cemetery.

MOUNT HOREB MUSTARD MUSEUM
**100 West Main Street,
Mount Horeb, Wisconsin**

Mount Horeb Mustard Museum is probably the most famous museum of its kind in the world. Visitors to the museum will find an incredible 4,400+ jars, bottles and tubes of prepared mustards from all 50 US states, and from more than 60 countries. The Gourmet Foods Emporium is another part of this fascinating place, and you can do more than just look here; you can taste and take home your choice from over 800 selections, which also includes other gourmet sauces and condiments in addition to mustards.

It all began in October 1986 when its founder, Barry Levenson, had just seen his beloved Red Sox lose the World Series to the New York Mets. Depressed, he went to an all-night supermarket and roamed the aisles. In the condiment aisle, at the mustard section, a voice seemed to say to him: "If you collect us, they will come". Barry bought a dozen different jars that night and resolved to amass the world's largest collection of prepared mustards. Keeping his day job as Assistant Attorney General for the State of Wisconsin, it was not until 1991 that he left to devote himself full-time to his passion of mustard collecting.

The Mount Horeb Mustard Museum opened to the general public in 1992, subsequently moving to its present site (which is across the road from the old one) in October of 2000. The museum collection has grown from its humble beginnings to now contain thousands of different mustards and hundreds of items of mustard memorabilia. It has been featured on the Oprah Winfrey Show, and showcased in numerous national magazines and newspapers.

National Mustard Day is sponsored by the Mount Horeb Mustard Museum, and the museum is also home to the campus of 'Poupon U' - America's College of Mustard. Apparently they have the finest curriculum that money can buy, offer several degrees, and boast a famous and rousing fight song that goes as follows:

Who needs Harvard, who needs Yale?
At Poupon U, you'll never fail!
Stanford, Princeton? Big mistake!
Poupon U's a piece of cake.

Phew, hot stuff! It could truly only happen in the USA. God Bless America.

PAPER AIRPLANE MUSEUM
**70 East Kaahumanu Avenue,
Kuhului, Maui, Hawaii**

Billed as the "World's Only Paper Airplane Museum", this establishment holds a collection of over 2,000 airplane models and kits in addition to photographs and artifacts that relate to Hawaii's aviation history, from 1910 to the present day. Examples come from around the world and range from those that are a mere postage stamp size, to huge models that have a wingspan in excess of 6ft. Planes must be made from a minimum of 95% paper products to qualify for display here.

The museum however also features the sublime creations of owner Ray Roberts, known as 'The Tin Can Man of Maui'. Almost all of his creations can be bought including his pride and joy - a model of the Concord Jet made using over 90 cans.

Find the Paper Airplane Museum at the Maui Mall in Kuhului.

'Shakers' of all shapes, sizes, and colours.

SALT & PEPPER SHAKER MUSEUM
Winery Square, Gatlinburg, Tennessee

The world's only salt and pepper shaker museum is found at Gatlinburg, Tennessee, gateway to the Great Smoky Mountain National Park. More than 17,000 salt and pepper shakers from all over the world - including some of the strangest you will ever see - are all on display here in enormous glass cases.

The creativity for some of the 'shakers' is amazing. There are pieces made of all shapes and forms, and out of everything from rock, glass, sea shells, wood, ceramic, eggs, and a plethora of other materials. Heaven only knows who thought all these shapes and forms up, but you simply must see the rooms upon rooms of quirky pieces at the Salt & Paper Shaker Museum. Its amazing.

THE INTERNATIONAL VINEGAR MUSEUM
Main Street, Roslyn, South Dakota

Now here's a museum with a difference - vinegar and related products from all over the world, including paper made from vinegar. Everything you always wanted to know about vinegar can be found at The International Vinegar Museum. You can taste vinegars, learn how it is made in both factories and villages, buy unusual vinegars, or enter the Mother of all Vinegar Contest at the Annual Vinegar Festival.

Vinegar's main ingredient is Acetic Acid which is sometimes called Ethanoic Acid. The chemical formula for Acetic Acid is CH_3COOH. This alone, however, does not constitute vinegar which is made from natural materials in a natural process.

MUSEUM OF COLORADO PRISONS
201 North 1st Street, Canon City, Colorado

Visitors here get the opportunity to explore the history of Colorado Correctional Facilities. See the hangman's noose that was used for the last execution by hanging in Colorado, the Federal Bureau of Prisons display, the gas chamber, and confiscated inmate weapons and contraband. Sit in the cell of Alfred Packer (America's favourite cannibal), see the exhibit of Anton Wood, who at 11 years old was the youngest person convicted of murder, or visit any of the other 30 or so themed cells with amazing exhibits. Great Fun.

SING SING PRISON MUSEUM
Ossining, New York

Gruesome thrills galore at the infamous Sing Sing Prison Museum which presents an unadulterated insight into imprisonment and correction. Your visit is made all the more scary when you realise that Sing Sing Prison itself is still functional, providing long-term accommodation for over 2,000 inmates that includes murderers, rapists and hoodlums.

An electric chair is on display, confiscated weapons can be seen still in their evidence bags, and a 'shank' can be seen which is an instrument made from 2 plastic forks bonded together, and intended to 'gouge' the eyes out!

The prison itself has many long-term inmates who never leave their cells, for fear of being killed. Such is Sing Sing.

TEXAS PRISON MUSEUM
491 Hwy 75, N.Huntsville, Texas

Texas Prison Museum traces the development of the Texas prison system from its beginnings in 1848 to today; a system that now has over 150,000 offenders and a couple of billion dollars budget. The museum's prize possession is the most famous electric chair of all time - Old Sparky - in which 361 prisoners were fried between 1924 and 1964. This chilling exhibit was in storage at the Walls Unit Death House before being donated to the museum, and interesting to note is that it was actually made by prison workers. Today, lethal injection is the method used when a death sentence is passed.

Many of the exhibits here give an accurate insight into the creative and alert minds of prisoners who manufactured weapons from materials found within the prison units. The Contraband Exhibit showcases improvised knives, lifelike guns, and even a ball made out of slivers of compressed paint. This would have been dropped into a sock and used to devastating effect. Drugs were highly sought after and one exhibit is a boot worn by a prisoner named Charles Harrelson. It has a hollowed-out heel in which he smuggled drugs. The Prison Hardware section shows the various types of equipment that were used to restrain or contain inmates. Padlocks, handcuffs, batons, and even a ball and chain can be seen. They were also punished with a fearsome looking instrument called 'the bat' which is also on display. The tubing and straps from the first lethal injection can be seen alongside the 'Teletype Machine', a TWX Model 33 that was used to receive last-minute reprieves.

Welcome to the
Texas Prison Museum.

Grim reminders of penal
time in years past.

The Still foreboding walkways of Sing Sing.

Old Sparky, America's most
famous electric chair which sent
361 people to their death
between 1924 and 1964.

- wood you believe it -

MUSEUM OF WOODCARVING
539 Highway 63, Shell Lake, Wisconsin

Internationally renowned, there are superb scenes and carvings at the Museum of Woodcarving, the largest collection of woodcarvings in the world. They are all the work of one man, Joseph T.Barta, and the museum features over 100 life-size biblical wood figures and in excess of 400 miniature carvings. The reproduction of 'The Last Supper' is a single example of his extraordinary work. Done in minute detail, it took him more than 4 years to complete. Other exhibits include Herod waving a wooden baby over his sword, and a wooden Judas dangling from a noose.

Apparently, Barta's work is the result of revelations in which he had a vision of Mary, and God is said to have told him what to do. Barta died in 1972 at the age of 68 but his work will live on for centuries. Incidentally, he made all his own glue.

DECOY MUSEUM
215 Giles Street, Havre de Grace, Maryland

Located on the banks of the historic Susquehanna Flats, the Havre de Grace Decoy Museum houses an enormous collection of working and decorative decoys. Over 2,800 decoys (mostly ducks) line the walls of the building which attracts bird lovers, hunters and tourists alike. Tours, lectures, and fully functional workshops enables interested visitors to learn all about the art.

The sport itself is called waterfowling and part of the collection is used in the Chesapeake area. Decoys have been part of Chesapeake culture for centuries and at the outset they had a single use - to lure waterfowl within the range of the hunter's gun. They were simple representations of ducks or geese, roughly carved from wood. These days you are as likely to find decoys adorning a wall or mantlepiece, and collectors snap them up.

A lovely tranquil setting greets you at this unusual, yet enchanting museum.

DEÅ MUSEUM
VISITORS ENTRANCE

HOURS OF OPERATION:
TUESDAY - FRIDAY
10:00 AM TO 4:00 PM

FOR MORE INFORMATION:
202-307-3463
WWW.DEAMUSEUM.ORG

DRUG ENFORCEMENT ADMINISTRATION MUSEUM
700 Army Navy Drive, Arlington, Virginia

The only museum in America devoted to drugs, drug abuse, and drug-law enforcement can be found in Arlington, not far from the Pentagon. The museum features interactive kiosks, exhibits on the history of illegal drugs in America, and has a literature corner that will fill you in on anything you need to know about acquiring a hallucination, without seeing the wife naked.

The exhibits include a mock-up of an opium den from the 1800's, an illegal crack house, and an old fashioned drug store. You can find out all about the 1960's drugs such as marijuana, amphetamines and psychedelics - to present day designer drugs like crack cocaine and heroin. Spaced out man!

JOHN Q.ADAMS CENTRE FOR THE HISTORY OF OTOLARYNGOLOGY - HEAD & NECK SURGERY
1 Prince Street, Alexandria, Virginia

For an offbeat museum try the one above (its too long to type again). It was founded to preserve the history of otolaryngology-head and neck surgery, promote research, and provide educational material for the profession and the public alike.

The collection contains much in the way of papers, research work, artwork and artifacts - but also some bizarre looking implements such as a Chinese ear-cleaning device. It resembles a pair of tweezers with 2 scrapers on a chain. Other exhibits include Hearing Aids Through the Ages, an Introduction to Tracheotomy, and Early Tonsillectomies. Another Virginian oddity.

MUSEUM OF SEX
233 Fifth Avenue (27th Street), New York City, New York

Titillation, education, serious art, or an outlet for the long raincoat with deep pockets brigade - there's something for everyone at the Museum of Sex. Although not a pornographic museum, visitors will see illustrations and pictures, statues, machines, and videos guaranteed to either stimulate the mind or other parts of the body. An immense porn collection donated by retired Library of Congress curator Ralph Whittington is quite astonishing. Since picking up a pocket size porn magazine on a school trip he 'came-out' as a collector over 20 years ago. His vast collection includes more than 700 videos, 1,500 magazines, numerous books, over 400 8-millimetre films, and a wide range of other sex related items such as blow-up dolls. Another collection on show is the abundance of sex-education videos from past decades which illustrate the dangers of unsafe sex and the perils of gonorrhea, etc. A collection of magazine covers seen at the museum featuring naked women are no different from those seen on a news stand, but they are meant to be representative of changing fashions and attitudes.

It has to be said that in addition to a lot to be seen, there is also a lot to be learnt at the Museum of Sex. A retrospective on American pornographic films - some dating back to 1915 - is particularly interesting, whilst US patented sex machines will either amuse or amaze you. There is even a preserved (presumably pickled) human penis here which even The Icelandic Phallogical Museum (featured in this book) does not yet have.

Sections on sex and the law, Stags, Smokers and Blue Movies which includes silent films, and Mapping Sex in America, all have a part to play in educating us on the history of sex and what it encompasses in America. Some of the anti-sex paraphernalia and artifacts to be seen that predate the 1960's can be quite startling but it is said that the museum's objective is to provide sexual education with an academic and historical viewpoint.

The Harmony Theatre was an establishment located at Broadway and 48th Street in Manhattan in the 1980's that re-enacted old style striptease. Promotional signs and much memorabilia from the theatre can be seen at the Museum of Sex as a reminder of those times.

One of the better displays at the Museum of Sex, and one that will certainly bring colour to your cheeks, is the US Patents Office Sex Inventions. The patents illustrate America's changing views about sex in culture and includes a variety of corsets that were designed to compress and shape the body in a multitude of bizarre ways, an old appliance that used vacuum and heat to draw blood to the penis (which was the opposite of the water cooled inhibitor of 30 years earlier), and a contraption that went around the penis and was attached to the pubic hairs with small clamps - the idea being that if an erection occurred during the night the clamps would tug on your pubic hairs and wake you up! Not very nice, but not half as bad as the Spermatorrhea Ring that was designed in 1862 and had extremely sharp metal points to discourage erections. Unbelievably, many of these devices actually made it into production and it makes you wonder what drives an

Please do not touch, lick, stroke or mount the exhibits.

museumofse**x**
NYC

inventor into making cruel devices to prevent people from touching their genitals, except to urinate.

From sex machines like the bizarre 'Thrillhammer' to a naked photograph of actor Yul Brynner, find them all and a whole lot more at this innovative museum. Sex and technology are entwined here as most of the exhibits are connected with technology in some way; there are many virtual exhibits as well as actual exhibits. Everyone has to visit this place at least once in their lifetime. Are you getting enough? You are now leaving page 69.

Strange signs (above) and strange sights (right) at the Museum of Sex in New York City.

MUSEUM OF FAMILY CAMPING
100 Athol Road, Richmond, New Hampshire

Are you ready for this? Roy B.Heise (1910-1991) had a dream. It was to open a museum and display his collection of camping memorabilia along with other items associated with family camping. The Museum of Family Camping is therefore dedicated to him and offers the rare opportunity for visitors to see such treasures as a campstove similar to the one Admiral Peary took to the North Pole, a Norwegian rucksack (1930), and a 1938 travel trailer. Other not-to-be-missed gems are reflector ovens capable of 600 degrees heat, a folding table that they say "will remind you of your uncle's roll-top desk", and an 1895 sleeping bag in remarkably good condition but weighing 10 times more than the modern version.

Audio-visual treats here include Camping-The Early Years - a 22 minute insight into family camping from the days of the Indian travois, past the Model T era, and through to the opening of the museum which was in 1993. There are taped stories and recounts of camping adventures told by campers from long ago, or numerous old photographs to look at portraying the earliest vehicles. Browse through the early camping magazines and books - some now said to be classics, or see the Early Tents and Fireplaces exhibition which will make you glad that Salvation Army hostels have been around a long time. There must be something to it all as this smallish museum, found amongst the pine trees, has featured on CBS This Morning, a national TV show.

The Museum of Family Camping state

that a visit to their Hall of Fame can be an "inspiring experience". This is a place that features portraits and photographs of some of its members, plus assorted plaques that detail their achievements. Apparently, "the bountiful occurences of today's family camping are the result of their vision and devotion. We owe them much". They go on to state that "enshrined here are all the greats of the past and the present who have furthered and enriched camping by giving of themselves without thought of personal gain". Hang on a minute, hasn't progress played a part in all of this?

Staffing, maintenance and renovation of historic displays are costly and drain the resources of the Museum of Family Camping. They invite you to become a part of the "museum support team". Hmmm. I suppose you do get to see the Indian-made Adirondack pack basket used by a trapper for more than 35 years, or the Maine guide's well-blackened coffee pot made for him by a 'tin-knocker' of 4 generations ago, as many times as you like. Oh, and don't forget the Northwoods primitive campsite (1955) that includes traditional dingle stick and a stump cut by beavers, complete with wood chips.

All of the above is true, honest.

Part Three
- REST OF WORLD -

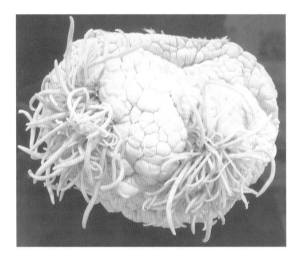

A preserved brain with a parasitic infection seen at
The Meguro Parasite Museum - page 89.

THE LAUNDRY MUSEUM
2-11-1 Shimomakuro, Ota-ku, Tokyo, Japan

There is an 8,000 volume library here completely devoted to laundry. The museum features laundry equipment from the last century and a whole host of items including irons, washboards, and even paintings (including those by Renoir and Picasso) that are in some way connected with laundry. Its true, and it could only happen in Japan.

Who would have thought it - a complete museum themed on laundry. Pictures left, and above, show just 2 of the old laundry exhibits on display at The Laundry Museum (Igarishi Kenji Kinen Sentaku Shiryokan) in Tokyo, Japan.

SULABH INTERNATIONAL MUSEUM OF TOILETS

Sulabh Gram, Mahavir Enclave, Palam-Dabri Marg, New Delhi, India

The Sulabh International Museum of Toilets urge you to join their 'Sanitation Crusade'. Apply on-line now.

There are museums themed on just about everything in this wide and wonderful world of ours, and this place ranks near the top of the tree of wacky museums.

It was Dr. Bindeshwar Pathak, the founder of the Sulabh International Social Service Organization (a non-profit business in the field of sanitation in India) who came up with the idea that there was a need for a museum of toilets. Setting about his task, he trawled worldwide to find out the various toilet designs that were in use in different countries, and at different points in time. Information, photographs and samples were gathered, and the museum can now claim to provide a detailed history of the historic evolution of toilets from 2,500BC to date. Find out about the technology, toilet etiquettes, and sanitary conditions of various time periods. If you want more, then admire the extensive display of chamber pots, bidets, privies and other toilet furniture.

In ancient times Britain created very ornately carved and painted urinals and commodes, whilst the mobile medieval commode, in the shape of a large chest, was used by the English when out hunting.

The chamber pot started out as a most plain and nondescript object, but during Victorian times in England it became an object d'art. It was seen as something that could always be improved upon and, in 1929, an American electrician patented an electric chamber pot which had an asbestos and rubber seat around the upper edge with metal bands embedded that enclosed resistance wires. This was thought ideal for cold nights. King Louis XIII actually had a commode under his throne, and sometimes gave an audience whilst using it. A replica of his throne and commode can be seen at the museum. Portable commodes, colourful commodes, strange commodes (such as one that looks like a bookcase), and a whole lot of other commodes are all on display here.

The museum has everything imaginable to do with toilets - from cisterns and urinals, to classic toilets with chain flushes, and all the associated fittings. They come in all shapes, designs and colours. many very beautifully decorated. In most museums you struggle to find a toilet, but not here.

The museum was established with certain objectives, some of which are; "to help sanitation experts learn from the past and solve problems in the sanitation sector", and, "to educate students about the historical trends in the development of toilets". Another fine objective of the museum is "to provide information about the design, materials, and technologies adopted in the past and those in use in the contemporary world". This is all very well but the simple fact of the matter is when you've got to go, you've got to go. The colour, shape, pattern and material that the toilet consists of never crosses your mind. You've just got to go.

Discover the secrets of authentic and traditional pasta making when you follow the signs to the National Museum of Pasta Foods.

Pot noodles galore. Its instant ramen at the Noodle Museum.

- oodles of noodles & piles of pasta -

SHIN-YOKOHAMA RAMEN MUSEUM - NOODLE MUSEUM
2-14-21 Shin-Yokohama, Kohoku-ku, Yokohama, Japan

Ramen (or noodles to us Westerners) is the caviar of Japan. You find it everywhere and most of the population are ramen connoisseurs and avid fans. The Shin-Yokohama Ramen Museum is no ordinary museum as it stays open until 11pm to cater for the hordes of hungry concert-goers leaving the nearby Yokohama Arena.

The first floor of the museum is entirely devoted to countless exhibits of every ramen connected product under the sun (thought this was the land of the rising sun). Instant ramen packets from around the world, old ramen commercials, ramen bowls, ramen-making utensils, wrappers, aprons, and even a replica of the first ramen dish ever eaten by a 17th century samurai called Mito Komon. There are even ramen-themed interactive games and a show about an instant ramen factory here.

None of the above will prepare you for the remainder of the museum which is located on 2 underground levels; a miniature historical theme park based on the year 1958 and containing restaurants, shops and houses, and a lot of nostalgic fixtures and fittings. Here, the serious ramen addict can choose from 8 ramen shops (which were selected from tens of thousands throughout the country), with all the major ramen capitals being represented - such as Sapporo and Kitakata. It has to be said that the food is superb and the experience is a memory that will last. Right, I'm off to the supermarket for a beef and tomato pot noodle.

NATIONAL MUSEUM OF PASTA FOODS
Piazza Scanderbeg 117, Rome, Italy

Oddio! Se l'avessi saputo, avrei cominciato a parlare italiano anni prima (Goodness! If I had known, I would've starting speaking Italian years ago). You really do need to speak the language at the National Museum of Pasta Foods in Rome, Italy (where else), as there's so much to ask - because I love spaghetti.

This is a serious museum for lovers of the Italian 'first course' as it holds seminars, publishes books, and is a main point of reference for scholarly enthusiasts.

There are various rooms to visit such as the Ligurian Room or the Wheat Room. The exhibition is a documentation of the evolution of pasta covering 8 centuries and pasta production takes centre stage here. Pasta in different shapes and strange forms can be seen, in addition to traditional styled pasta products. Not only the history, but also the methods of production and machinery used (including some very ancient examples) are examined and seen here.

Find the National Museum of Pasta Foods at the foot of the Quirinale Palace, near to the famous Trevi Fountain. Ciao.

THE ICELANDIC PHALLOGICAL MUSEUM

Hedinsbraut 3a, Husavic, Iceland

Its not all wee willie winkie's at The Icelandic Phallogical Musem in Iceland. There are many large specimens including the monstrous 5ft 2in organ that once hung proudly on a sperm whale (twice as long when it was still attached). It is now preserved in a cylinder of formaldehyde. Visitors to the museum will see a collection of about 250 penises and penile parts belonging to all the land and sea mammals found in Iceland, and representatives from around the world.

It all started in the 1970's when Sigurdur Hjartarson was given a whale penis by a friend who worked at a nearby whaling station. When word got around, other people started giving him penises, and so his collection began. Today, the museum exhibits over 30 specimens belonging to 12 different kinds of whale, about 20 specimens from 7 different kinds of seal and walrus, and numerous specimens from countless other animals. Goats, dogs, bears, cats, and even the rare aquatic unicorn all have their dangly bits on show here. Some strange willies include those from a tanned bull that was once used as a whip on a farm, and a smoked horse's todger that was said to have been a prized dish in the 1930's. This is a showcase for the diversity of mother nature's endowment distribution to the animal world and is not for the faint hearted. There are no human penises - for now, but several men have bestowed their reproductive organs (penis and scrotum) for the empty human section of the museum. One of these has requested that his tackle be removed from his body whilst still warm, thus giving the museum the opportunity to exhibit it erect.

All manner of strange specimens relating to the genital organs of the male of the species can be see here including pickled penises floating in jars, penis bones, dried fibrous penises, and stuffed penises. There are also some fantastic curiosities to admire such as the doors with willie shaped handles, and many phallic orientated ornaments and oddities, including utensils. The gift shop sells some hilarious items that make for gifts with a difference. Skipping ropes with phallic handles, coat-racks with penis pegs, and even penis-styled salt and pepper shakers.

Although the museum offers the opportunity for individuals to seriously study the field of phallology in a scientific way, it is mainly curiosity seekers who make up the majority of the visitors. The Icelandic Phallogical Museum is located in a small fishing village of about 2,500 inhabitants (since its move from Reykjavik). It is only a few miles from the Arctic Circle meaning most of us will never see this world of wonderful willies.

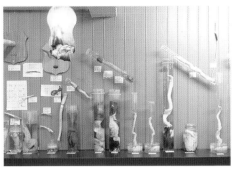

Specimen jars containing all sorts of penises and associated bits at the tittilating Icelandic Phallogical Museum in Husavic, Iceland.

There are dozens of penises in all shapes and sizes (above left) adorning the walls of the world's only willie museum, including some of the biggest around which belong to types of whales.

Phallology is an ancient science which, until recent years, would only have been practised in connection with another discipline such as biology. Scientists of today group mammalian penises into 2 types; animals such as bulls, sheep and horses have a fibroelastic penis which is semi-erect all the time and is fully controlled by muscles. Other mammals, such as monkeys, polar bears and humans, have a muscular cavernous penis which becomes erect only upon the inflation of spongy tissue. Many of these are equipped with a retractable penis bone, although humans do not have one of these which

means we cannot 'break' our penis.

Following the results of a scientific paper it is believed that the Arctic environment leads to an evolution of long penis bones due to high latitude. Animals that live in high latitudes are more likely to copulate with as many partners as they come by, as cold weather means they would have trouble meeting mates. By virtue of this, a male who can deposit his sperm deeper into a female than his rivals is much more likely to pass on his genes. A longer penis bone is evidently more useful in these circumstances.

Notorious, convicted serial killer Charles Manson (above) and (below) the violent shooting of mobster Albert Anastasia at a New York City barber shop. Both reproductions, together with many more, can be seen at the Criminals Hall of Fame Wax Museum.

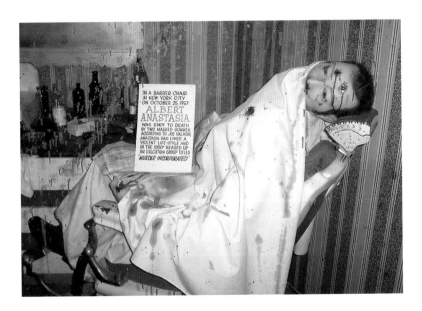

MEIJI UNIVERSITY MUSEUM OF CRIMINOLOGY
1-1 Kanda Susugadai, Chiyoda-ku, Ochanomizu, Japan

The Meiji University Museum of Criminology was established in 1929 to archive criminology records, and there are more than 250,000 items stored here. Japanese torture techniques were not subtle, but you can also see guillotines, iron maidens, and any other manner of inscrutable devices that were intended to severely punish, not only in in Japan but also in other countries.

In Japan's Crime and Punishment section there is a chronological display of a variety of old historical laws, whilst the Culprits of the Edo's Period, Torture and Tribunal, and Execution and Correction exhibitions all give a full account of a history of supressed human rights. Some of the artifacts are quite gruesome.

The musem hopes that through this type of criminological history, visitors (mostly Japanese) will gain a deeper appreciation of human dignity. We call it 'trying to put the frighteners on you' where I come from.

The Meiji University Museum of Criminology is in the Soritsu Hyakushunen Kinen Daigaku Kaiden building (bet the names lengthways on it) on the corner before the Liberty Tower. It gives a good account of the severity of punishment meted out in the days before Japan was more open to the rest of the world. Well worth visiting should you ever find yourself in this part of Japan with a few hours to kill.

CRIMINALS HALL OF FAME WAX MUSEUM
5751 Victoria Avenue, Niagara Falls, Ontario, Canada

Some of history's most notorious criminals are recreated out of wax here in creepy, realistically presented bloody tableaux, which are all behind glass. Almost all are from the United States and there is gore aplenty, which will satisfy even the most demanding blood and guts enthusiast.

Convicted serial killer Charles Manson who is said to have never actually killed any of the victims himself, Timothy McVeigh in his orange prison suit, gangster Al Capone, and head of 'Murder Incorporated', Albert Anastasia can all be seen here together with dozens more The highlight comes at the end - an electric chair that buzzes when you sit in it. One of the better wax museums.

MUSEO CRIMINOLOGICO - CRIMINOLOGY MUSEUM
San Jose, Costa Rica

The museum is located in the building of Supreme Court and has exhibitions of weapons, drug related items, counterfeit money and lottery tickets, and the tools of past crimes. There are many grotesque and bizarre pictures including black and white pictures showing quartered bodies, and even actual body parts on show here. The narration of the history of criminology and law enforcement in Costa Rica is quite compelling.

MUSEUM OF QIN TERRA COTTA WARRIORS AND HORSES
Xi'an, Lingtong County,
Shaanxi Province, China

It was the 29th of March, 1974, when farmers of XiYang Village, Ling Tong County, were drilling wells in search of water, that ancient bronze weapons were discovered. At once, the head of the village reported the finds to the local government. On the 17th of July that same year, an archaeological team from Shaanxi Province arrived to excavate the site and began to unearth the most significant archaeological find of the 20th century. What was discovered was a collection - although many would say an army - of life-size terra-cotta figures of warriors, horses and chariots near the mausoleum of the First Qin Emperor; Qin Shi Huang of the Qin who established the first feudal dynasty in Chinese history. They were buried there to defend him in the afterlife.

Incredibly, work is still ongoing to this day at the site. The mausoleum covers a total area of 20 hectares, and there are 3 main buildings of this museum, (named pits) that these historic finds are assembled in. Pit 1 is a huge arch-domed steel structure covering 16,000 square metres and containing over 1,000 terra-cotta warriors and horses in battle formation. They were displayed there soon after restoration. The lines of soldiers are arranged in 10 columns separated by reinforced earh mounds, with the soldiers at the front and the war chariots at the back. Pit 2 and Pit 3 were brought to light in 1976, with Pit 3 eventually opened to the public in 1989, and Pit 2 opened in 1994.

Pit 2 is 20 metres northeast of Pit 1 and contains over 1,000 warriors and 90 chariots of wood. Pit 3 lies 25 metres northwest of Pit 1 and seems to be the command centre of the armed forces. It contains about 100 warriors, a war chariot, and several horses.

Altogether, well over 7,000 pottery soldiers (terra-cotta is a waterproof ceramic), horses, chariots, and weapons have been unearthed. Some have crossbows and many are in kneeling positions, whilst others stand behind to shoot over their heads. The majority have protective armour and almost all have been restored to their former glory.

About 60 million people have visited the museum and in some quarters it is referred to as 'the eighth Wonder of the World'. It is certainly one of the most spectacular discoveries of all time and is now listed by UNESCO as one of the World Cultural Heritages.

Upon ascending the throne in 246BC at the tender age of 13, Qin Shi Huang had work started on his mausoleum. It was a project that took over 11 years to finish. He later became the First Emperor of China and it is speculated, following his death, that many buried treasures accompanied him to his afterlife.

The size of the army of terra-cotta warriors which were buried to protect both his journey to, and in his afterlife, were indicative of his all powerful position as the First Emperor of China.

The amazing terra-cotta warriors - thousands of them - representing the most significant archeological excavations of the 20th century.

TOBACCO & SALT MUSEUM
Shibuya-Ku, Tokyo, Japan

For lovers of quirky museums, look no further than the Tobacco & Salt Museum in Tokyo. With the non-smoking brigade at their loudest in America and Europe, and government legislation against smoking starting to bite at the ankles, did someone forget to tell Japan - as they actually celebrate and relish the art and relaxation of puffing away in a big way.

The Tobacco and Salt Museum specialises in collecting and studying materials that are relative to both tobacco and salt, and the public show their appreciation for the quality of the exhibitions held here by turning up in droves.

It was around 1600 that tobacco turned up in Japan and it soon led to a whole new culture. The plant and its uses are implemented in a variety of ways, but smoking it is still the firm favourite. The museum's selection of Japanese pipes on display, wonderful artistic paintings of smokers, and cigarette packs and packaging from around the world are all interesting to see.

Salt has been around even longer than tobacco, and a visit to a Japanese Ryokan for a bowl of extremely salty Miso soup will perfectly illustrate its popularity level on a par - if not above - that of tobacco in the land of technological advancement. Salt is essential for life, and despite having no worthwhile natural sources of the product, over the years Japan has produced sea salt and has a sophisticated salt technology.

No matter that tobacco and salt are 2 infamous commodities, Japan's love affair with them is unlikely to diminish in the forseeable future.

Tokyo's Salt & Tobacco Museum
- once monopoly goods in the country -
extols the virtues of both product.

GERMAN HYGIENE MUSEUM
Lingnerplatz 1, Dresden, Germany

Learn everything you always wanted to know about health and hygiene at the German Hygiene Museum, which was built for the 2nd International Hygiene Exhibition that was held in Dresden in 1930. This is a museum that focuses on hygiene in relation to the human body - not disinfectants and scrubbing worktops. It is said to be one of Europe's most interesting science museums and certainly has a novel approach to the way the themed exhibits are treated.

The permanent exhibition revolves around the human being, and the way they deal with aspects of human life. Living and Dying is one of 7 themed room. It charts the progress from the first cell created to a person's eventual death. Remembering, Thinking and Learning, is a study of the cosmos of the human brain. The Transparent Man shows images of the human being in relation to modern sciences, whilst Sexuality is an in-depth look at the love, sex, and way of life in relation to reproductive medicine. Other themed rooms are to do with things such as beauty, skin, eating, drinking, etc. What putting together an 'Invisible Man or Woman', or looking at a life-size version of a gall bladder has to do with hygiene, is your guess as well as mine.

The original focus of the museum until 1990 was on conventional information on health. Scientific developments since then has caused a radical rethink, and seemingly a change of direction - although the original name of the museum remains the same. The exhibits here are certainly life-like, and it is a hands-on learning place that will appeal to many.

CULTURAL HISTORY OF THE HAND MUSEUM
Am Brunnen 1b, Wolnzach, Germany

Another strange museum from the land of frankfurters, this time about the 'cultural history of the hand'. This originated as a private collection owned by a local businessman and most of the collection is shown at the museum today.

Although the museum's name may seem somewhat strange, its contents and displays explain all - and fascinate you. What you see here is a thorough and revealing insight and history of the hand in all its uses. The 'wonderwork' hand is explored in 7 different showrooms. Speaking Hands addresses hand attitudes and gestures, and how they convey messages between human beings. The Hand as a Symbol looks at the various ways hands have been used in advertising, on coins, or as decoration. Artificial Hands is quite interesting as it looks not just at prosthesis, but also at mechanical hands or robots. Mysterious Hands explains the old magical practice of hand reading called Chiromantie. We'll skip the rest as you probably get the gist.

It is said that the hand, and its unique construction, enables it to fulfill the function of a fine motor - being precise and like a highly sensitive instrument. The museum attempts to cover all aspects of use that the hand could possibly be put to. I can think of a few popular and important uses that are not covered by this well presented museum. One is nose-picking. The other one (usually performed left-handed) we won't go into here.

GUANAJUATO MUMMY MUSEUM - MUSEO DE LAS MOMIAS
Explanada del Panteon, Guanajuato, Mexico

The Guanajuato mummies were discovered in a cemetery in the city of Guanajuato, which is northwest of Mexico City. An old local law in the area required relatives to pay a form of 'grave tax'. You could pay the tax once (170 pesos) and that was that, or pay a yearly fee (20 pesos) that was more affordable, and would have appealed more to less wealthy families. If the yearly tax was not paid for 3 consecutive years the body was dug up from the cemetery and placed in a repository, which is now known as El Museo de las Momias - the Mummy Museum. If a deceased person's family had moved from the area, or perhaps they were the last in the family line, it mattered not. The law was the law. All this occurred between the years of 1896 and 1958, when the law was changed. No new bodies have been exhumed since then but the museum still displays the original mummies.

The mummies (107 of them) are somewhat a mystery due to their remarkable condition. This could possibly be attributed to the soil conditions and the dry climate of the mountainous area which would have caused the bodies to dry out in a natural way, before they could decompose. Whatever, the Guanajuato mummies are some of the strangest ever to be seen on display. Some still have clothes or shrouds, a few have only socks or shoes on, but most have looks of pain or horror on their faces. Some are old whilst others are children. One very small baby mummy has been named "La Momiamas pequena del Mundo" - the smallest mummy in the world. The baby and its mother (they died during a caesarean section) are both in the museum.

It is rumoured that some of the mummies suffered mysterious deaths or were the victims of horrifying crimes, although there is little evidence to support this. However, one mummy is that of a woman who is said to have been buried alive. The Mummy Road Show hosts viewed the mummy and said this theory was supported by the fact her arms were raised over her face, and her forehead had scratch marks. Apparently no scientists have studied the mummies.

These 'modern mummies' attract plenty of attention. Tour buses regularly arrive at this tasteless museum which is high on a hill overlooking the city. Nobody knows for sure how they were preserved in such a way, and it is uncertain how many more lie in the cemetery in a similar condition. Surely there is no need to display them in such an undignified and horrific manner, but to give them a decent burial where they may find peace the second time around.

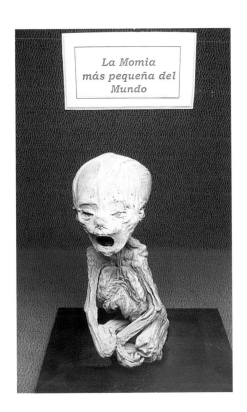

Gruesome, but compelling. Possibly the most horrific museum in the world is the Museo de las Momias (Guanajuato Mummy Museum). Over 100 mummies are on display here, many strange and grotesque, including (above left) "La Momia mas pequena del Mundo" - the smallest mummy in the world.

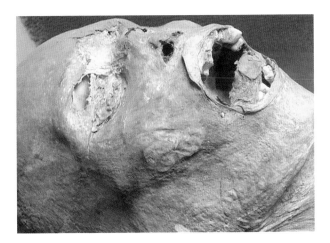

EUROPEAN ASPARAGUS MUSEUM

**Am Hofgraben 1,
Schrobenhausen, Germany**

Asparagus, the 'royal vegetable', has its own dedicated museum in Germany covering 3 floors of a tower in an historic city wall. It is said that Schrobenhausen was the site of the first asparagus planting in Bavaria, and it is celebrated at the European Asparagus Musem in many ways. Find out what the common asparagus pests are, ways of preparing it, and all about the use of asparagus in medicines. Asparagus paintings, asparagus tips (hee hee), and everything you need to know to further your mind in respect of asparagus. If you are dining out here then the local white asparagus is very good, and served with most meals.

Germany has more speciality food museums than most European countries. Heichelheim is home to the Dumpling Museum which is the Thuringians' national dish. Made from the potato, this has been served up in Thuringia since the 17th century. The history of the potato as well as the dumpling can be found at this museum.

The Horseradish Museum at Baiersdorf, the home of horseradish, is where you can discover the hottest of all local condiments. As stated by them; "Marvel at tales and stories all about horseradish, and at the products in the museum shop. Experience the world of the magic root".

The Bread Museum in Ulm, where over 14,000 objects can be seen, has received well in excess of a million visitors since opening its doors. The peppermint museum at Eichenau is always popular, and there is a Sugar Museum and a Curried Sausage Museum in Berlin.

So what is the attraction of these seemingly average, offbeat museums? Well, regional food culture plays a big part, and food culture in general is a way of life in Germany. Or perhaps there is another connection. At the Spice Museum in Hamburg they hold special exhibitions and events that look into the aphrodisiac effects of certain spices. These are always well attended. Meanwhile, over at the Chocolate Museum in Cologne they are conducting special guided tours themed 'Women Need Chocolate'.

SALVATORE FERRAGAMO SHOE MUSEUM
Palazzo Spini Feroni, Florence, Italy

In a career that spanned over 40 years, Salvatore Ferragamo designed over 10,000 shoes until he died in 1960. Examples of most of them can be seen at the museum. There are striking, stunning, and bizarre examples of Ferragamo's work here in addition to Marilyn Monroe's stiletto heels, Audrey Hepburn's shoes, and many more pairs of celebrity footwear.

Books, photographs and sketches illustrate many of the finer points in the design process of shoes, whilst highlights to look out for include the shoes made from dyed fish skins, and sandals covered in 18 carat gold and pearls.

THE BATA SHOE MUSEUM
327 Bloor Street West, Toronto, Ontario, Canada

This is a most unique shoe museum housed in an award-winning 4-storey building which has a most unusual frontage. It was the creation of architect Raymond Moriyama. Celebrating the style, function, and changing attitudes to footwear, The Bata Shoe Museum has over 10,000 shoes, plus artifacts and footwear-related items to be seen.

Egyptian sandals, Chinese bound-foot shoes, and chestnut crushing clogs are some of the examples of old international footwear to be seen. There is always a special exhibition taking place which may cover such themes as Oriental Footwear, Celebrity Shoes, or Historical Footwear.

Find The Bata Shoe Museum at Bloor Street West in Toronto. The building is unmistakable.

BEPPU HIHOKAN
338-3 Shibuyu Kannawa, Beppu City, Oita Prefecture, Japan

Hihokan means 'palaces of secret treasures', and there are many of them in Japan over all 3 islands. They are basically a version of Europe's sex museums - only more explicit. If you are unprepared then what you will see in a Hihokan will certainly shock you, and any misconceptions you may have had about Japanese people being reserved and coy will be shattered when you see what lies within. Most advertise themselves with flashing neon lights and colourful, yet gaudy exteriors.

The Beppu Hihokan was founded by a collector of sexual artifacts in the 1980's. Inside there is a bizarre mix of exhibits and displays ranging from the dildos and x-rated videos behind glass cases at the entry, to the Snow White exhibition where she can be seen being sexually attended to by the 7 dwarves. There is a huge 9ft wooden penis to see in addition to many shelves of smaller ones in all kinds of twisted shapes and forms. Some of the exhibits are quite bizarre; female mannequins pose in themed scenes dressed in bondage gear, silk, fur and the like. One has a cigarette in her hand and a dog in front of her. When you press the button the dog's head goes back and forth pulling at her panties.

Another section of the Hihokan museum has a comparison of penis sizes, whilst everywhere you look there seems to be copulating dummies (or dolls as they are called) in various stages of sexual activity, and in some mighty inventive positions. The movie theatre here has a porno film on a loop so you can endlessly watch the same 3 girls taking turns with a solitary guy - in about 12 different positions.

Most would view Hihokan places as harmless titillation and, certainly, the Japanese people themselves prove this as couples and groups of women are the most frequent visitors. Having a laugh is the same in any language. There is however a dark side to it all as some of the Hihokan sites accommodate various acts and demonstrations of bad taste. The Big Horse Show is held sporadically where, if you've the inclination, you can watch 30 or so horses as they mate.

There is a kind of serious educational side to all of this. Japanese historical art, which takes in many forms of the erotic, can be seen at most Hihokan. At the Beppu Hihokan they have a superb collection of ancient woodblock prints which leave little to the imagination.

Kazuhito Kawashima, of the Tokyo Soken Architectural Company, is a bit of an icon in the Hihokan world. He has designed many of these erotic palaces and looks on the Hihokan as an adult museum, or amusement park that adults want to visit. These places are not cheap and cost a pretty penny to set up. Kazuhito says that you need 200-300 million yen per building, and each of the dolls (the copulating dummies or mannequins) costs about 4-5 million yen. Apparently he has also built miniature Hihokan for theme parks across Japan.

Hihokan, or sex museums, are as popular as saki, tobacco or salt in Japan. Perhaps its refreshing that they have a more open attitude to sex and eroticism than many countries, though where a smiling Snow White getting a leg-over (14 to be precise) comes into it is anyone's guess.

THE MEGURO PARASITOLOGICAL MUSEUM
4-1-1 Shino Meguro, Meguro-ku, Tokyo, Japan

Perhaps not the ideal place to visit if you've just eaten dinner, but The Meguro Parasitological Museum is a must-see place in Tokyo. This is a proper research institute that educates as well as giving you the shivers. Here you will find that 6% of all animals from the 70,000 species are parasitic, and 300 of them you can see here. Cockroaches, lice, mosquitos and all manner of fearsome looking small beasties can be viewed in close-up.

Metre-long tapeworms make you wonder just what could be lurking in your body, but when you see the almost 9 metre specimen here, then you'll be extra cautious over what you eat in future. It was taken out of a man after he ate raw trout. He found its head sticking out when going to the toilet one day. The pictures on show include men with elephantitis, and a man whose scrotum almost touched the ground after getting an infection in his testicles.

The second floor gift shop is where you can buy all the sort of parasitic gifts that will not appeal to those with a squeamish nature. One charm bracelet has 'Diplozoon Nipponicum' set in it - which to you and me is a parasitic freeloader that lurks inside cold fish.

All manner of nasties lurking in specimen jars at the Meguro Parasitological Museum, the world's only parasite-dedicated museum.

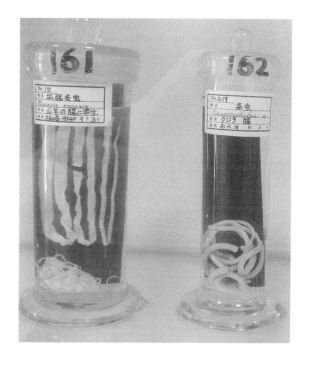

- bells and balls -

THE BELL MUSEUM
Innsbruck, Leopoldstrasse 53, Austria

The Grassmayr family has been casting bells to sell worldwide for over 400 years. Bells are cast and constructed using age-old customs of traditional craftsmanship and the museum is a combination of Sound Room, Bell Foundry, and Bell Museum. The Sound Room is an acoustical adventure that will satisfy the most discerning ear. Visitors are invited to partake in this experience. The Bell Foundry illustrates the art of traditional bell-making where you can see skilled craftsmen plying their trade. The Bell Museum tells you everything about the history of bells and is a most entertaining journey through the centuries. Exhibits and memorabilia can also be seen.

NAPTHALAN MUSEUM FOR THE CRUTCHES OF CURED PATIENTS
Napththalan, Baku, Azerbaijan

Napthalan is a small town in Azerbaijan but is a major health resort because of the unique Napthalan oil which is extracted from borewells here. Napthalan oil is used for curing certain diseases such as those connected with the skin, peripheral nervous system, and gynaecological disorders amongst others. It also possesses local anti-inflammatory and anaesthetic properties.

Napthalan can also lay claim to having the strangest museum in the world; one dedicated solely to the crutches of cured patients. The opening hours are not known but I doubt you'll be going to Azerbaijan to see it anyway.

- lot of bottle -

BOTTLE PETER MUSEUM
Smedegade, Aero Island, Denmark

Aero Island is a sleepy 6 x 22 mile island on the south edge of Denmark. Secluded beaches, thatched and half-timbered cottages, and several 5,000 year old neolithic burial grounds are some of the sights that greet visitors. The island has a timelessness to it and probably the busiest place is the harbour at the capital, Eroskobing. Here, frequent visitors are are mainly Danish and German holiday yachts.

The sleepy island is also home to an unusual museum. At Smedegade visitors will find the Bottle Peter Museum in a fascinating house. Most of us have seen ships in bottles and wondered how they got there, and here you will see a huge collection of 750 of them in all shapes and sizes. They were the creation of Peter Jacobsen who made his first bottle at 16 and his last at the age of 85. He often bragged that he drank the contents of each bottle before setting to work on his fleet of bottled ships (except those that contained milk), and he died in 1960. Visitors may be few and far between but this is a little gem of a museum that visitors should seek out, if only for the curiosity factor.

After your visit to the Bottle Peter Museum look at some of the tombstone engravings to be seen throughout the island. They contain such sentiments as; "here lies Christian Hansen at anchor with his wife. He'll not weigh until he stands before God".

You have arrived at the Bottle Peter Museum - home of 750 different bottled ships. How did the ships get in them?

AMSTERDAM SEX MUSEUM
Damrak 18, Amsterdam, Holland

Right in the middle of a very busy tourist area on Damrak, Amsterdam's main street, is one of the city's most popular tourist attractions - the Amsterdam Sex Museum. This is not to be confused with the nearby Erotic Museum which is nowhere near as informative.

The museum is always packed with visitors (mostly curious couples) and has 3 floors heaving with displays ranging from the erotic to the exotic, and the burlesque to the bizarre. Moving mannequins and recorded voices can sometimes be quite startling; one mannequin says "psst", and then flashes at you, whilst a huge naked woman suddenly appears out of the shadows of an alleyway in the old Red Light District.

Meant to be informative in an educational way, the museum houses an extensive collection of international historical erotic, and pornographic art that includes countless pieces in addition to much literature. Manuscripts and drawings can be seen from the Karma Sutra to erotic 20th century comics. Explicit Japanese carved ivories and Greek temple items with a sexual twist are part of the international items on display, all indicative of the relation of eroticism and sex with art, religion, and more. Every object in the collection is well documented to include the approximate date, country of origin, and how it was used if necessary. This all seems harmless enough and even some of the mannequins exhibited here are merely postured in a titillating manner. But all of this is in stark contrast with some of the other stuff to be seen, much of which can surely have no place in a serious establishment. Does a plastic bottom that farts and giggles when you go past it really play a part in the history of sex?

Much stronger stuff here includes one room on the first floor that contains photographs devoted to the extremes of sex. Bondage, fetishism, group, anal, and even bestiality is seen here. There is a sign warning you not to complain should you choose to enter. The Amsterdam Sex Museum also has a huge photographic and film library that contains every sexual preference and predilection known to man. Displays of old black and white photography from private collections can also be seen together with paintings, statues and the like, again from either private or professional collections.

An interactive section entices visitors into a choice of several small padded booths. Inside, a selection of films play continuously and there's no prize for guessing what you will see.

There is certainly much to see here including contemporary paintings which you can view whilst sat on traditional chairs, or on one of a pair of realistic looking, 7ft penis and testicle shaped exhibits.

This museum is inexpensive to visit and will satisfy the serious sex connoisseur, the casual voyeur, or those looking for a an injection of humour into their lives. The Netherlands is noted for its very liberal views on sex and sexuality and that is very evident in this popular museum. 'Doggy' does not mean 'come here rover' at this place.

*Relax at the Amsterdam Sex Museum and admire the erotic art
or simply watch the world go by. Sit on a traditional chair or
perch on the nut-sack of a 7ft tall penis exhibit. Careful though,
one of these vibrates and is likely to put the willies up you!*

PARIS SEWERS MUSEUM
**Pont de l'Alma,
93 Quay d'Orsay, Paris, France**

The sewers of Paris have been handling wastewater since the beginning of the 13th century when the streets of the city were paved, and drains were constructed by order of Phillipe Auguste who was the King of France from 1180 to 1223. Today's network of sewers in the French capital cover over 1,300 miles and work on the tunnel network was begun in 1850.

Until recent times the sewers also carried tourists - initially by carts that were suspended from the walkways above the walls, and later on in carriages pulled by a small locomotive. Boats were also in use up until about 1970.

After paying to get in you descend into a long gallery that is underneath the Quai d'Orsay (running parallel to the River Seine). This was once a main sewer line and a 5-ton 'flushing boat' can be seen here. You will also see large basins that trap solid material from the wastewater, and some amazing things get pulled out.

The main exhibit area of the museum is the Belgrand Gallery which is further along. Huge wooden balls used to clean sewer tunnels, mannequins of sewer workers, sewer maintenance equipment from the past and present, and exhibits telling you all about the history of the Paris sewer network all provide much information that you may, or may not, want to know. The sound of rushing water is everywhere on this interesting tour, and you may even see the odd rat. Clothes-pegs for your nose are optional.

SEWER MUSEUM - SIELMUSEUM
20359 Bei den St, Pauli-Landungsbrucken 49, Hamburg Germany

The Sielmuseum is a collection of objects that have been fished out from the Hamburg sewerage system. Although these tours have to be booked in advance it is well worth it to see the diversity of things that somehow find their way into the land of pee, poop, and rainwater. Buttons, coins, false teeth, artificial limb, and even a birth certificate and bicycle are some of the items that have been recovered. There is also a display of historical cleaning equipment on show.

One of the many exhibits at the Zeppelin Museum in Friedrichshafen.

ZEPPELIN MUSEUM
Seesstrasse 22,
Friedrichshafen, Germany

Friedrichshafen is famous as the home of the Zeppelin. Industrialist Count Ferdinand Graf von Zeppelin (1838-1917) invented the concept here and the town has a memorial in his honour. The main attraction at Friedrichshafen is the enormous Zeppelin Museum which is located on the promenade of Lake Constance. It contains the world's largest collection of airships, ranging from the very first to the very latest Zeppelin, and covers 43,000 sq.ft of exhibition space. Here you can experience the history, technology, and some would say glamour of airships and zeppelins.

There is a reconstruction here of a 108ft long section of the legendary

LZ129, or Hindenberg as it was known. This can be seen complete with passenger lounges and crew rooms. One room at the museum concentrates solely on the use of Zeppelins in the Great War. There is much memorabilia to be seen here including the engines that powered these majestic wonders of the sky, crew uniforms, and equipment, etc.

From 1900 until World War II, the town of Friedrichshafen on Lake Constance was known as 'Zeppelin City'. During that period it was the main manufacturing centre for these huge airships and, although its production focus shifted somewhat following World War II, it soon returned to its speciality production and unveiled a new transport airship - the LZ-N 07. On the 2nd of July 1996, the 96th anniversary of Count Zeppelin's first airship flight, the Zeppelin Museum was opened.

book orders & suggestions

We hope you have enjoyed reading this book and will want to purchase other titles of Strangest Books. Please see the back cover for a brief description of other titles currently available in this series.

Our books can be purchased from all good book shops and a broad selection of other retailers. Alternatively, you may wish to visit our website where excerpts and images from other titles can be viewed free of charge, and books may be ordered direct.

We are always interested in hearing from readers with any comments or suggestions. If you would like to contact us please use the relevant e-mail link below.

e-mail direct

bookorders@strangestbooks.co.uk

suggestions@strangestbooks.co.uk

or visit our website at:

http://www.strangestbooks.co.uk